# BRAVE

# SEAMEN

## OF

# YOUGHAL

### &

## Other Stories

---

Mike Hackett

LOCAL HISTORY COLLECTION
ON STREAM

Published 1995 by On Stream Publications Ltd. Currabaha,
Cloghroe, Blarney, Co. Cork. Ireland. Tel/Fax 021 385798
© Mike Hackett
ISBN:1 897685 92 0

This is a Youghal Credit Union Community Project

Cover photograph: Mike Delaney taken by Michael McKeown

Acknowledgments:
Michael T. Murphy Chairman UDC.
Rev Dean St. John Thornhill PP.
Rev Peter Rhys-Thomas
Gay Byrne, RTE
Colm Keane RTE
Devonshire Arms Hotel
with thanks for their assistance with the launch of this book.

Barry Treacy, Manager Youghal Credit Union, his staff and all the
directors, for their great goodwill and support; Lieut. Commander
Laurence O'Sullivan, naval archivist, for his encouragement and
assistance; Tadhg Kelleher, Hon. Sec. Youghal RNLI for his great
co-operation; Patrick Aherne for his memories of life at sea; Captain
Pat Walsh, MNI, AMIPR, author & journalist, for his successful fact-
finding and help; Michael O'Brien, Maritime Historian, for his great
contributions; Kevin Melly, Tall Ship enthusiast for his unselfish
supply of photographs; Thomas B Williams, Maritime Researcher
for his help; John Schofield, Computer Expert, who saved this
book, despite my efforts to lose it in bytes.

ACKNOWLEDGMENTS Brendan Ahern, Frank Ahern, (London), Martin Boyle, Betty Buchanan, Ivy Coleman, Francis and Geraldine Casey, Billy Collins, Jim Corr, Matty Coakley, (London), Edmond Cooney, (Los Angeles), Johnny Coyne, Eamon Cronin, (Sligo), Noel Cronin, Michael Cullen, Nora Connery, Michael Connor, Denis Collins, George Daly, Noel Donoghue, Vincent Fitzgibbon, Tom Flavin, Catherine Fleming, Ned Foley, Ray Gordon, Vivian Halfpenny, Anthony Hannon (Los Angeles), Billy Healy, John Hickey, Joe Higgins, Dan Hogan, (Plymouth), John Kiely, Kitty Lane, Paddy Linehan, Willie Lyons, Brendan and Martin Maher, (London), Denis McCarthy, John McGrath, Nora McGrath, Liam Mulcahy, John O'Brien, Michael O'Brien, Billy O'Connell, Fidelma O'Connell, Marian O'Halloran, Anna O'Neill, Jack (Leanbh) O'Suilleabháin, Eileen O'Sullivan, (Ballybofey), George Perks, Gerald Pomphrett, Eileen Power, Leonard Power, Frank Reilly, Willie Roche, Cecil Roy, (U.S.A.), Kitty Ryan, Margaret Sweeney, Donal Scanlon, Mabel Shortall, Mary Ann Smyth Willie Walsh. and Mrs. M. Harvey-Williams.

Irish Lights. Youghal and Kilmore Quay Branches of RNLI. Gus Smith, for the use of his book on the 'Arandoro Star', and remembering Des Hickey, Co-Author of that book. John Young for his Maritime History of Dungarvan, Field Printers, for the use of 'Hayman's Annals of Youghal', and The Marine Times (Killybegs). And fondly remembering, - Dan Fleming, Ted (Black) Healy, Terri (O'Brien) Keyes, Kathleen Mulcahy, Ashe Street and John Ryan all of whom helped to prepare this publication but who have since gone to their reward.
Ar Dheis Dé Go Raibh A n-Anamnacha.

# Contents.

# Introduction.

Over the centuries, vessels swarmed the local quays to bring goods from abroad like coal, slates, timber, salt, spices and beer. Exports were butter, grain, fish, beef, pork, wool, pelts, iron, timber, bricks and earthenware. English merchants, prior to 1810, had their ships from Bristol call here for beef, pork and fish on their voyages to Newfoundland. All this sea commerce encouraged local adventurous youths to sail away in search of their fortune.

Many never returned to their hometown for different reasons and it is time to record those who died on their travels. Tall-ships, tossing helplessly with their sails furled or in tatters, foundered without trace. Others were driven onto rocks and wrecked, especially before the major lighthouse building programme of the mid-nineteenth century. Later, and most shocking, was the terrible loss of life at sea during the wars from shelling, torpedoes, aircraft attack and mines. In the old days when a man died at sea, far from land, he was wrapped in canvas and buried in the deep (Davy Jones locker), and so we see little trace of these in graveyards. A few more died and were buried in foreign ports as far apart as Rio de Janeiro in Brazil and Archangel in Russia. Thus, far away from home and then sometimes almost on our doorsteps, our men of the sea died without creature comforts. The first part of this book is an appreciation of those men. The second half celebrates the land and the characters I had the privilege to know or hear about before they are forgotten without record. I offer this small contribution of Youghal's local and maritime history and anecdotes for your pleasure.

Mike Hackett

*They that go down to the sea in ships and occupy their business in great waters; these men see the works of the Lord and His wonders of the deep.*
Psalm 107

# The Development of the Port of Youghal.

Youghal as a port was exporting clay for pottery-making in very early times, even before its fine harbour was formed when the river Blackwater changed course in the ninth century. This resulted from severe thunder and lightning which caused the swollen river to break it's southern banks and gush for the sea through what is now Youghal Harbour. The projecting Ferry-Point is a reminder that the land stretched the whole way across a marshy valley in bygone times. Until then it joined the sea via Piltown, Bawnacomera and into Whiting Bay near Ardmore.

We start with Saint Declan at Ardmore, the saint who founded his seminary there in 416 AD, when it was on a headland which overlooked the mouth of the Blackwater. It was typical of settlements established at great rivermouths, acknowledging that the best mode of transport then was by water. Perhaps if the river had not changed course, Ardmore/Whiting Bay could now be a single large port while Youghal might be only a little one.

When the Danes first came to plunder this area they must then have entered the Blackwater via Whiting Bay, before going upriver to raid Molana Abbey at Dair-Inis (Isle of the Oaks) and Lismore. It is also believed that religious houses near Clashmore were raided and the occupants killed. The new rivermouth location meant that Eochaill or Youghal now became the focus of attention for shipping.

Hayman's 'Handbook for Youghal' (Field's Printers) tells us about the Norwegians (Danes) building a fortress at Eochaill where they also laid the foundations for a large seaport. Then in 864, a ferocious sea battle took place in

Youghal Bay during which a fleet of the Desi defeated the Danes and the fortress was destroyed.

Later, in the the twelfth century, another sea battle was fought between the Irish and Normans in Youghal Harbour. Strongbow's men had travelled downriver from Lismore, with their boats full of loot, but had to wait at the harbour-mouth for a favourable wind to sail them to Waterford. In the meantime, 32 barques from Cork arrived to intercept them and the two fleets engaged in deadly battle. The outcome was in favour of the Normans, mainly because the stone slings and battleaxes on the Cork boats were no match for the cross-bows of the invaders.

During the Crusader Wars, a ship carrying fighting monks from the Knights Templars of Rhincrew sailed out of the harbour for the Middle-East. Then, early in the fourteenth century, three fighting ships were demanded of Youghal for the King's war against the Scots. It was the only Irish port from which three vessels were sought. By comparison, the others were : Drogheda, Dublin and Waterford, one each ; Cork and Ross, two each.

So famous was Youghal that in the 'Annals of the Four Masters', Cork was referred to as 'a place near Youghal'. 1650 saw Cromwell leave Ireland from here on the 'President', having sacked many Irish towns, killing thousands. Then, a century later, the port was reaching its busiest period with hundreds of vessels visiting there every year. Trade was done with England, France, Germany, Holland, Spain, Scandinavia and across the Atlantic with North America. Youghal was, at this stage, catering for a large area of Munster and later a plan was drawn up to supply towns as far upriver as Mallow using flatbottomed boats. This would have entailed building a number of locks on the Blackwater in different locations. It never came about and the arrival of the railway system killed the plan.

Often ships in the harbour were too numerous to count as they anchored off awaiting a berthing place at the quayside. Green's Quay, Allen's Quay, Green's Dock (Buttimer's), Steamer's Quay, Harvey's Dock, Pier Head, Market Dock, Nealon's Quay and Mall Dock would all be jammed with vessels of different sizes.

The waterside was busy with hundreds of men, on ship and shore, working themselves beyond tiredness. They toiled, barefoot, barely clad, in singlet and trousers. Baskets of coal, barrels of fish, lengths of timber and boxes of butter were moved manually with the aid of primitive rope systems. Unions and workers rights were unheard of and only fit, healthy, hard-working men were taken on by the shipping agents to run up and down the gangplanks. People without a breakfast on the first hiring day would pretend to be well fed and energetic so as to get a job. Then some of the merchants insisted on the hired man's family buying the groceries from their own shops as part of the hiring deal. While working together shoremen rubbed shoulders with sailors and heard about foreign lands of plenty and opportunity.

Shoremen then joined ship to see for themselves, and a large number from Youghal lost their lives to the sea as storms and wars took their toll. An old sailor told me that when he first went to sea as a boy, his father was a seaman on board the same ship. On the first day out, the sea was smooth as glass and looking very attractive. The father called his son over to the rail and pointed down to the water. "Don't trust it, son, and remember always that the sea is your worst enemy".

There were ships, regular visitors to this port, whose crews were well known and felt at home here. Sailors like **Captain Jewell** and **Philip White**, of the 'Kathleen and May' are remembered. Philip died on board in 1958.

It was a brigantine, 'Dei Gracia', later to become a Youghal vessel, which discovered the famous 'Mary Celeste', drifting unmanned, but otherwise intact, off the Azores. 'Dei Gracia' was American registered at the time and was carrying barrels of turpentine from New York to Genoa. A few crewmen went aboard the deserted 'Mary Celeste', before both ships sailed into Gibraltar where it was hoped to claim salvage. The inquiry dragged on, unfinished, for three months before the 'Dei Gracia' sailed for Genoa to deliver its cargo.

Moving down the Italian coast it took on a cargo for London, where in turn it took on railway chairs for Liverpool. Arriving in Merseyside, the captain and crew received the bad news that the owners could no longer fund the ship. The three months idle in Gibraltar had been too much. The vessel was then bought by Flemings of Youghal who used it to bring coal across the Irish Sea.

These sailing ships had to make for shelter at the first sign of a storm and while once doing so, the 'Dei Gracia' met a headwind on its way into Milford Haven. Trying to judge the right amount of canvas to use, the velocity of the wind and the amount of channel available made tacking into a headwind a supreme effort. It was to prove too much even for the very experienced crew and she went onto the rocks. There she remained, jammed but not wrecked. All six men were safely taken off. They were Captain **Joe Aherne,** First Mate **Patrick Aherne, John McGrath, Willie Evans, Dan O'Keeffe** and **Willie (Wally) Donoghue.**

Lloyds were asked to examine the ship and the cargo was transferred before she was towed clear and taken for repair. **Tommy Murray** of Cobh was the next owner when she was subsequently used as a bunker for the bigger vessels. Then came the building of Haulbowline shipyard during the First World War and she played her part, though by now her life was coming to a close. The end came for the 'Dei Gracia', when she was sunk to support one of the piers at that Haulbowline project.

Jimmy Delaney, fisherman, beside the 'Lord Nelson' at Green's Quay
*Pic: Tom Bulman*

# Epitaphs from Old Headstones in North Abbey.

Sacred to the memory of Captain Thomas Hayes of Dungarvan who died July 22nd. 1832 aged 78 years.
"The port is reached, the sails furl'd
Life's voyage now is o'er
By Faith's bright chart he has found that world
Where storms are felt no more."

Of your charity pray for the soul of Thomas Flynn Junior who perished at sea, March 3rd. 1845 aged 20 years.

Erected by John McCarthy in memory of his son John who was drowned at sea in 1860.

Sacred to the memory of Captain John Sullivan and Margaret Wilson of the schooner yacht Echo who were drowned in Youghal harbour on the 4th Sept. 1861.
This tablet is erected by the Honorable Moore-Smyth as a small token of regard and esteem.

Maurice Fitzgerald, lost at sea in September 1891.

The 'Ceres'

# YOUGHAL SHIPS 1848.

| SHIP | CAPTAIN | REG. TONN. |
|------|---------|-----------:|
| ALCEDO | McCarthy | 115 |
| CHARLES | Henlon | 185 |
| CYRUS | Major | 52 |
| ELIZA | McCarthy | 123 |
| ELIZA ANN | Richards | 102 |
| ELLEN | O'Keefe | 109 |
| EUPHEMIA | Kettel | 48 |
| FANNY | Williams | 123 |
| FANNY PENNY | Hegarty | 87 |
| FORESTER | Pendergast | 73 |
| HARRIET & JUNE | Sheehan | 109 |
| HOLLY HOW | Major | 116 |
| JOHN | J. Vincent | 127 |
| MARY HOUNSELL | Pendergast | 112 |
| MARGARET | Stannistet | 142 |
| PERFECT | Loughlin | 111 |
| PETER & MARY | Gibbons | 94 |
| REBECCA | Tullock | 119 |
| SALLY M | Carey | 75 |
| SUSAN GREEN | Lloyd | 186 |
| WILLIAM PENN | Coffey | 103 |

# The Call of the Sea.

What thoughts were harboured by sons of lost seamen as they braved the stormy ocean despite the sorrow and hardship it had already inflicted upon them? The old people used to say "The sea was in their blood", which was as near as could be to understanding it. "The call of the sea" was another phrase often used but that same cruel sea invariably meant more sadness. Grandsons felt the calling in their veins and sailed away out the harbour as the generations had done before them.

But angry breakers did not pick and choose as they dwarfed tall-ships, which wallowed helplessly under their empty sticks (sailors' term for masts without sails). Think of the womenfolk. Of a woman who lost her father, brothers and then her nephews to the whims of the sea. A young wife became a potential widow as she waved her husband goodbye. What magnetic power drew these men to the vessels? Was it a sense of adventure to travel and explore? To seek their fortune? Just to make a living? Or was it some kind of overpowering telepathy, as yet unexplained?

Of course the vast majority of seamen lived to tell the tale and went on to succumb to death quietly in their beds at a ripe old age. Even so, very few of those life-long sailors would have got through without having survived a few narrow escapes of one kind or another. The dangers were numerous, frequent and the mood of the merciless sea could be deceptive.

Many families were badly hit by misfortune on the water. **Connie Glavin** was drowned while salmon fishing in Youghal bay. His son, **William**, died serving on a minesweeper off the Cork coast in 1917 and the loss of the 'Nellie Fleming' in 1936 cost the life of another son, **Batty**. His two grandsons, **Connie** and **Eddie**, were lost in 1943 during the Second World War. Three generations were thus severely hit. **Tommy Smith** of Primrose Lane was another who was drowned while salmon fishing and later his son, also named **Tommy**, was lost from a ship at Rouen in France. The brothers, **Patrick** and **Johnny Brennan** from the Mall, were also lost to the water when.the former died on 'HMS Laurentic', which hit a mine in Lough Swilly in 1917. Johnny drowned in Youghal harbour in 1933.

 **Brendan Murphy** of Market Square was lost by U-boat action during the Second World War and his nephew, **Teddy**, died in 1962 from appendicitis poisoning which developed at sea. **Declan Doyle** of Pender's Lane drowned when the 'Nellie Fleming' disappeared, and his brother **John** was washed overboard two years later in 1938, going through the Red Sea on his way to Australia.

 Youghal Port meant a lot to the local people with its great employment in bad times, and related industries like fishing and boatbuilding were also careers into which local boys could go. But it was to sail the 'Ocean Blue' that most youths chose, sooner or later, and the cost in lives to the community was shocking.

 The pain was greatly felt during the war at sea 1939-45, when so many young men from Youghal gave their lives. The priest at Mass on Sunday would read out the list of deaths for the week which sometimes included teenagers who had left home just a few weeks earlier. No words can describe the terrible sense of loss which was suddenly thrust on those families.

 Across from the Mall, on Monatrea Hill, is a cottage which housed the Flaherty family about a hundred years ago.

There were two fishermen brothers in the family, and nearby were two Mulcahy brothers. Around the corner, at Eastern Point, is a little beach called Mangan's Cove where the rollers can be huge as the currents of the river and ocean come in conflict. The **Flahertys** and **Mulcahys** were said to have been very brave fishermen and it was here that their boat capsized, drowning the two pairs of brothers. Such was the show of sympathy in the area, that the four coffins were shouldered all the way to Grange burial ground, six miles away.

The 'Asecurador'

The 'B.I.'

# Misfortune at Sea.

In February of 1936, the 'Nellie Fleming' needed a cabin boy to double as cook and two youths applied for the job. **Eddie Sullivan** and **Eddie Norris** were both hopeful of starting a seafaring career on the 'Nellie'. Eddie Sullivan got the job and sailed away to Wales with four other crewmen while the other Eddie, very disappointed, stayed at home. On the return journey, the Nellie left Lydney laden with coal on a calm evening in that February of 1936. However, as she sailed away from the Bristol Channel, the weather changed. A storm was brewing.

The 'Kathleen and May' was also heading for home at the same time, but unlike the 'Nellie', it was a sailing ship with an auxiliary engine. So the 'Kathleen' decided to drop sail and motor for port and in the small bay of Angle, in Milford Haven, it found shelter. The 'Nellie', with sail only, ran helplessly before wind and tide. On board were five crewmen, all from the home port: **Captain Michael Duggan**, married, a very experienced sailor; **Batty Glavin**, married, who was returning to his daughter's wedding; **Dan Kenneally**, married, with a large family; **Declan Doyle**, an eighteen year old, and **Eddie Sullivan** of Raheen Road on his first voyage. The wind that night was fearful as it built up to record an average of seventy-five miles per hour for the whole of the next three days. It became the worst storm in living memory on the Irish Sea.

Meanwhile, back in Youghal, the people feared the worst for the two vessels. Down on the quays, crowds kept vigil, saying the Rosary for the safe return of their loved ones. Nine days later, the 'Kathleen' rounded the Eastern Point, to be greeted by a big cheer that could be heard across the harbour.

There was relief for some and hope for others. "Any sign of the 'Nellie'?" they asked. "No sign" was the dreaded reply. But the vigil went on. Then word came from Dungarvan that a storm damaged ship had come in there. A car was hired to quickly drive the eighteen miles over the Drumm Hills to the neighbouring coastal town. But no, it was not the 'Nellie'. Again, from Dunmore East, came word of a sighting and another car sped off. Still not the missing Youghal schooner! No trace was ever found. The 'Nellie Fleming', without an engine, was no match for that terrible storm. Five lives taken together shocked the town so much, that even now, our elders can still feel the indescribable sadness.

Shortly afterwards, in 1940 and 1941, the town was to be saddened again when the sinkings of the 'HMS.Glorious', 'HMS.Galathea' and 'HMS.Barham' each cost several local lives. During 1940, the Aircraft Carrier 'HMS Glorious' was ordered to proceed homeward from Norway because of fuel shortage. She was escorted by two destroyers, 'HMS Arden' and 'HMS Acasta'. The carrier was not flying normal air search patrols, so was caught unawares by two German battle-cruisers and sunk by gunfire. Only three officers and forty men were saved out of a crew of 1,200. 47 RAF men on board were also lost. **Miley Long, Jack Murphy** and **Tommy Stack**, all from Youghal, died on the 'Glorious'. The two escorting destroyers attacked, but although they scored one torpedo hit, they were themselves battered and sunk with just two survivors from the 'Ardent' and one sole survivor from the 'Acasta'.

On 25th. November 1941, a U-boat got through the destroyer screen and fired four torpedoes at the battleship 'HMS Barham', off Sollum in Egypt. It was at point blank range, so close, in fact, that the massive secondary explosion blew the submarine (U-331) to the surface. In the resulting confusion the attacker got away. The 'Barham' disappeared in four minutes, taking 862 men with her. **Jerry Connolly** and **Bobby Webster** were two of those. They were both stokers and had no chance as they worked in the bowels of the ship.

The cruiser 'HMS Galathea' was hit by a U-boat torpedo off Alexandria just after midnight on 14th. December 1941. Out of 508 crew, 380 were lost, and 128 were saved. In that sinking, the lives of **William Kirby** and **Brendan Murphy** were taken.

In 1942, while **Maurice Hickey** was in Scotland, he received a telegram from Dublin asking him to return for a job that awaited him on the 'Irish Pine'. Maurice was delighted and made arrangements to go back across the Irish Sea as soon as possible. Sea transport was irregular because of the danger of attack, with the result that Maurice arrived late. The 'Irish Pine' had already sailed to cross the Atlantic, so he was disappointed. A fellow townsman and good mate of his, **Alfie Hartnett**, had sailed out on the ship. A few days later the 'Irish Pine' was torpedoed and sunk in the North Atlantic. An additionally sad fact was that Alfie Hartnett, who was lost, had been married to **Mamie (Webb)** for only six weeks when he was taken so tragically from her.

The Head-of-the-Rock (Moll Goggin's) corner is the commanding viewpoint out over the sea from the main road (N-25). It is to this spot that the sister of a lost sailor goes, every time she comes home on holidays. "I know that he is somewhere out there on the ocean ", she lovingly and sadly says as she remembers his young face from almost sixty years ago.

Long ago, oars were used to propel the fishing boats, but you could also have had a single mast to hold a sail in favourable winds. This would have been used to travel longer distances, like that from Ardsallagh to Youghal, to sell fish, and back again. It was while approaching Bridge Quay (Metal Bridge), using a small sail, that a boat capsized causing the deaths of four local fishermen from Ardsallagh. They were named as **Maurice Fleming, William Keating, Maurice Keogh** and **John White**. Ardsallagh is a small, hill-dominated townland which is cradled on three sides by the horseshoe course of the Blackwater. The river is strong and wide here as it gushes to the sea, just three miles away. Easy to understand then how closely knit that small community was, semi-isolated, as on any peninsula. Easier again to imagine the grief as four young men were 'waked' within a few hundred yards of each other. It was on Palm Sunday 1892, that the four coffins met at Ardsallagh cross for the last solemn journey to Clashmore.

When the brigantine 'Citizen' was wrecked on the south side of the small Saltee Island on 23rd. December 1895, the entire Irish coast was witnessing a particularly violent spell of weather. At Youghal, wreckage from the 'Eaglett' of Chester was washed ashore and the White Star liner 'Majestic' bound from New York to Liverpool could not land passengers or mail at Queenstown (Cobh). At Kingstown (Dun Laoghaire) the lifeboat capsized drowning fifteen of its crew in appaling conditions while on service to the barque 'Palme'.

The chain of events that led to the Kilmore Quay lifeboat being launched began when a local man first spied the 'Citizen' at 1.15p.m. on 23rd. December with her sails flapping, rolling heavily at the back of the Small Saltee. A fearful gale was blowing, creating a very heavy sea at the time of discovery. The lifeboat 'John Roberts' was launched into the teeth of the storm and after two and three-quarter hours pulling against the south-west gale, it reached the stricken brigantine. Great risk was taken to bring the crew to safety.

Unfortunately **Captain Michael Lynch** and **Patrick Bowler** lost their lives. The lifeboat took the four survivors to Kilmore Quay village, where they received food and clothing from the hospitable locals. Their condition, for a while, gave cause for some concern after their terrible ordeal. However, due to the exceptional care received, the four recovered and, as soon as they were able to travel, the Chief of the local Coastguard gave a sum of money to pay their way home to Youghal. The following piece appeared in The Cork Examiner at the time -

*"For the past few days considerable anxiety was felt in Youghal concerning the brigantine Citizen, owned by Flemings, which left Cardiff with a cargo of coal on Saturday morning last. On Thursday night news was received that she had been driven ashore near the Saltee Islands and that the Captain and one crew member had been drowned. Both are serious losses as the Captain, Michael Lynch, and the seaman, Patrick Bowler, leave wives and families behind. "*

Windbound at Youghal 1938 *Pic: Horgans*

# Seamen of Youghal Who Lost Their Lives All Over the World.

Just when they had almost slipped out of memory, the trade winds seem to have whispered their names and so we fondly and respectfully remember them. God rest all their souls.

**Captain Fleming**, of Youghal died on the Schooner 'Hertford', shipwrecked on the Wexford coast in about 1882. It was owned by the Flemings, who were local Merchants and the Captain was one of the family.

**JAMES Butler** of Windmill Hill also died on the Schooner 'Hertford'. James was a baker by trade and this was his first voyage. **Patrick McCarthy** and **Seaman Bennet,** both of Youghal, were also lost on the same Schooner.

**Walter William Burke** of Hanover Street contracted Yellow Fever on the 'Melanope' in 1894. He died at sea and the ship went into port at Rio-De-Janeiro to bury him.

**Miko Loughlin** of The Mall died on the Schooner 'William S. Green', shipwrecked on the Devon coast in 1904.

**Danny Coakley** of North Main Street and **Tommy Walsh** of Mary Street both died on the 'William S. Green'.

**Jack Smith** of Flemings Court died on the 'Annette' when she went onto the rocks beyond Youghal Lighthouse in 1905. **Captain Kirby** of Dungarvan died on the same occasion.

**Patrick McCarthy** of Mouse Street (Ashe St.) caught a disease on a Brigantine in 1907, died, and was buried at Archangel in Russia. He was the grandfather of Noel Donoghue of Cross Street.

**Paddy O'Brien** of Ballyvergan was lost overboard from the destroyer 'Cossack' at Ayr, Scotland in 1919. He slipped on a steep gangway and struck his head on the quay wall whilst falling.

**Captain Patrick Donovan** of Strand Street died of blood poisoning on the 'B.I' at Runcorn, Merseyside in 1914 at the age of 32.

**Martin Bland** of Church Street died on ship in 1920 and was buried at Aruba in the Dutch Carribean. He was father of the late George Bland, Nile Street.(O'Rahilly St.).

**James Duggan** of Church Street was drowned while the Schooner 'Elizabeth Drew' was berthed at New Ross in 1933, in an attempt to rescue a fellow sailor.

**William Perrot** of Wales was drowned in 1933 while attempting to swim ashore from the Ketch 'Daisy' in Youghal Harbour, Upper.

**Tommy Smith** of the Alms Houses was lost overboard at Rouen in France in 1933.

**William John Coleman** of Quay Lane died aboard ship in 1936 on the way to Australia. He was buried at sea.

**Captain Michael Duggan** of Church Street was lost on the 'Nellie Fleming', which foundered without trace between the

Bristol Channel and Youghal in 1936. Also on the same vessel were **Batty Glavin** of Cork Hill, on the way home to his daughter's wedding; **Eddie Sullivan** of Raheen Road, on his first voyage; **Dan Kenneally** of The Mall, father of a large family and **Declan Doyle** of Pender's Lane, eighteen years of age.

**William Ring** of 135 North Main Street was lost overboard in Cardiff Docks in 1937. Having managed to hold onto a rope all night in the water, he later died from exposure.

**John Doyle** of Gallagher Terrace was lost overboard while on a voyage to Australia in 1938. He was a brother of Declan, lost just two years before on the 'Nellie Fleming'.

**Connie Troy** of Windmill Hill was electrocuted while repairing his fishing boat at Cobh in 1946.

**Michael O'Regan** of South Cross Road was serving in the Irish Naval Service on the 'LE Cliona' in 1952. He took ill on board and was brought to hospital, but sadly died at just eighteen years of age.

**Patrick Sullivan** of South Cross Road was lost overboard in 1962 at Newcastle-on-Tyne.

**Teddy Murphy** of Kent Street was struck with appendicitis at sea in 1962 on the 'Ordinance'. He died in Dunkirk Hospital.

**Tom Paul Ring** of Sarsfield Terrace died while sleeping in his bunk on the 'Irish Sycamore' as it lay docked in New Orleans in 1965. Smoke inhalation was the cause of death when a fire started in an empty cabin next door to his. **Joey Gaule** of Mall

Lane was a victim of the same fire.

**Gerry Griffin** of Brown Street was lost overboard from the 'Mossville' at Cork in 1967, when a plank gangway collapsed. Left behind were his wife and young family.

**Noel O'Brien** of DeValera Street was lost overboard from a dredger on the Thames in 1968.

**Joe Higgins** of Strand Street fell between vessel and quay at Greenock in Scotland in 1970 and was drowned. The ship was the 'MV St. William'.

**Timothy J.(Ted) Harnedy** from Inchiquin, Killeagh was drowned in 1982 while swimming at Bondi Beach in Australia. He was a ship's Radio Office on leave, awaiting a plane home.

**James (Jessie) Collins** of Raheen Road, died on the tanker 'Rathcoyle' in 1994. Asleep in his bunk while docked at Ellesmere Port near Chester, he died from a heart attack.

The SS Shark unloading fish barrels at Pier Head.
Spratts with salt & bayleaves were packed into the barrels.
*Pic: Horgans*

# Fishermen Who Died in River, Harbour and Bay Tragedies.

**James Hannigan** of Wesley Place, drowned when a salmon yawl overturned in Youghal Harbour in 1886. **Connie Glavin** of Green's Quay, was also lost in that same incident.

Two **Flaherty** and two **Mulcahy** brothers of Monatrea, were drowned when their salmon boat capsized at Mangan's Cove, in 1887.

**Maurice Keogh**, was drowned with **Maurice Fleming, William Keating**, and **John White**, all of Ardsallagh, when their salmon yawl capsized near the Metal Bridge in 1892. They were using a dip-and-lug sail at the time with which it was difficult to change tack.

**John Hogan** from Ardsallagh went for a swim in 1916 at the high rock near Fleming's Ferry, between fishing the tides, and it cost him his life. He had his passage booked to America at the time and a suit of clothes was being made for him in Youghal by a tailor called Bride.

**Tommy Smith** of Primrose Lane, was lost in Youghal Harbour in 1923 when his salmon yawl capsized. With him, and also drowned, were **Pats Murray** of Monatrea, and **Tom Aher** of Porter's Lane, Friar Street. Saved that day was Mike Hannigan, who for years was Cox of the Lifeboat.

**Bob Foley** of Water Street was drowned when another salmon-yawl capsized in 1927.Also lost then were **Declan Kenure** of Windmill Lane, and **Jim Boland** of Water Street

**John Brennan** of The Mall died in 1933 when yet another boat capsized on the river. Drowned with him was **Tommy (Truxie) Griffin** of Mill Road. Rescued on that occasion were **Tommy Heaphy** and **Mike O'Neill**.

**Mick O'Brien-Stokes** of Sarsfield Terrace died of a heart attack while in his boat salmon fishing down the harbour in 1949.

**Paddy Barry** from Ceann an Bhóthair (Clonard), received head wounds when his boat overturned in 1954. He died of his injuries in hospital.

**Declan Hannon** of South Main Street was lost overboard from a fishing boat in Waterford Harbour in 1972.

**Danny Twohig** of Blackwater Heights suffered a heart attack while hauling his nets in 1992 and died in the boat.

The 'Happy Harry'

# Lost at War.

The war at sea cost Youghal a number of lives. **Patrick Brennan** of The Mall died when the 'HMS.Laurentic' hit a minefield off Malin Head in 1917. Three other townsmen were drowned with him: **William Lynch** of Buckley's Lane, South Main Street, **Jacky O'Brien** of Windmill Lane, and **John Buckley** of The Mall.

**William Glavin** of Windmill Hill was lost when the minesweeper 'Mignonette' was torpedoed off the Cork coast in 1917.

**Tommy Stack** of South Cross Road, **Miley Long** of Water Street, and **Jack Murphy** of South Main Street died in 1940 when the aircraft carrier 'HMS. Glorious' was sunk by battlecruisers in the North Sea.

**Brendan Murphy** of Market Square, and **William Kirby** of The Mall, died on the cruiser 'HMS. Galatea' when it was torpedoed and sunk off Alexandria in 1941. It sank in ninety seconds.

**Jerry Connolly** of Cork Hill, and **Bobby Webster** of Sarsfield Terrace died when the battleship 'HMS. Barham' was torpedoed and blown up off Sollum, Egypt, in November 1941. The two Youghal men were stokers down below and had little chance of escaping the four torpedo hits. The second bigger explosion, when the ship's magazine blew up, ruled out any hope of survival.

**Tommy Roche** of Water Street died aboard the armed trawler 'Lincoln City' when it was torpedoed in the North Atlantic in 1941. He is buried on the Faroe Islands.

**Jimmy Walsh** of Raheen Road lost his life early in the war when his ship, a Merchantman, was sunk by a torpedo. It is said that in his home was a picture of a sailor returning from sea with his bag over his shoulder and his family greeting him. On the night that Jimmy was killed, the picture fell off the wall for no apparent reason. On inspection, the cord was perfect and the nail had not left the wall.

**Bill Kelly** of Market Square was killed when his vessel the 'Swiftpool' was bombed while moored on the Thames.

**Maurice Cooney** of Kent Street on another Merchantman was killed by U-boat action in 1941.

**Tommy Mulcahy** of Market Square died on the 'Kingston Hill' after it was torpedoed in 1941 - he was engaged to be married.

**Johnny Ronayne** of South Cross Road in the Merchant Navy was lost as a result of U-boat action in the early part of the war.

**Edward Fowkes** of Ashe Street was on the 'Shakespeare' during an aircraft attack on the ship. He was killed on deck.

**Peter Lynch** of Church Street lost his life when the 'SS Milos' was torpedoed and sunk in 1942. His parents later lived in the house which had been the Fever Hospital at Raheen Road.

**Alfie Hartnett** of Barry's Lane was on the 'Irish Pine' when it was sunk by U-608 in the North Atlantic in 1942. He had been married for only six weeks.

**Connie Glavin** of Cork Hill died when his ship, the 'SS Miriam Thomas', was run down while in convoy by an American transport ship in the Irish Sea. There were no survivors of that calamity.

**Eddie Glavin** of Cork Hill (Connie's brother) was killed when his ship was sunk by torpedo, three days out of New Zealand, in 1943.

**Michael Lynch** of Kent Street fell ill on board his ship 'SS British Renown' in 1944 and died. He is buried on the Isle of Wight.

**Paddy McGrath** of Strand Street died when the 'SS Empire Heritage' was sunk by a mine in 1944. He had survived two previous sinkings by torpedo in the North Atlantic.

*MAY THEIR CRAFT BE STRONG, THEIR CANVASS FULL AND GOD GO WITH THEM.*

There is a plaque in North Abbey bearing an appropriate prayer

*"Hail Mary, Mother of Graces, Patroness of Youghal,*
*We place ourselves, our homes, our town and country under your protection.*
*Grant that in our voyage through life, we will never founder on the rocks of evil,*
*But with a steadfast faith, a buoyant hope and a deep love of your son Jesus Christ*
*You will guide us to the safe anchorage of our heavenly home.*
*Our Lady of Graces, Pray for Us."*

Composed July 1984, by Fr. Tom Paul Geary, whose mother was one of the seafaring Glavin family.

The 'Nellie Fleming' of Youghal. Lost with all hands Feb. 1936  *Pic: Horgans*

The 'Kathleen & May' at Green's Dock (Buttimer's). *Pic: Horgans*

The upper photograph is taken from a Christmas card sent by Jerry Connolly on board HMS Barham to his family mid November 1941. A few days later it was hit and sunk by four torpedoes off Sollum. Jerry and another Youghal man, Bobby Webster, were amongst the 898 who died from a crew of 1218. The Connolly family of Cork Hill were told of Jerry's death on Dec 12th., just before the arrival of that card.

*Lower pic:* HMS Barham explodes – *courtesy Imperial War Museum*

The crew of the 'William S. Green': Miko Loughlin, Jimo Loughlin, Tommy Walsh, Dan Coakley.

Headstone in the Military Cemetery, Parkhurst, Isle of Wight.

Michael O'Regan's funeral at North Abbey March 1952. Officer Joe Higgins, Strand Street, leads the procession. Joe was later lost at Greenock, Scotland in 1970.

# Not Just Ordinary Seamen.

**James 'Dano' Troy** was a mighty strong fisherman, sailor, and footballer. We watched him come and go in all weathers, at times soaked to the skin, having been out all night but with no fish to show for it. In the off-season he worked discharging the vessels at the quays, in and out of the ships with baskets of coal, getting into the rhythm of the bouncing plank for fear of falling off it. On the necks of such workers could be seen the welts caused by the friction of the heavy baskets over many years.

Dano, in sport, was an outstanding footballer for Youghal and went on to wear the Cork jersey several times. He was in the Royal Navy during the Dardanelles campaign, when thousands were killed at Gallipoli during the First World War. For his time spent there, he received the princely sum of one pound and ten shillings every three months.

A self-educated man, he was knowledgeable in fact and fable, and loved to tell the children about the Headless Coach, the little Fairy Queen who perched on a stone at the top of Mall Lane combing her hair, the Mermaid of the harbour and of course the Banshee.

For years he manned the lifeboat and, at one rescue, a freak wave washed him out of the boat. He prided himself in the fact that the next wave returned him to within its reach, whereupon his brother, Mossie, grabbed hold and pulled him back in. "*When I was a sailor,*" said Dano, "*we had timber boats sailed by iron men. Now you have iron boats carrying timber men*". The gentle giant died at the age of 86 years, still bearing his own beautiful white teeth. There is an old saying 'Happy is the corpse that the rain falls on'. Dano must have been very happy because he was buried during the worst downpour that ever hit North Abbey. He was a legend in his own time and a large chunk of the quayside fabric was taken from us on that 26th day of September 1966.

Sailors Batty Mulcahy, James Dano Troy (seated) & Paulie Power.

James Dano Troy on Armistice Day.

While researching the lives of the seamen who were lost to the sea out of Youghal, the name of **Patrick Francis** kept cropping up. He and his brother **Harry** went to Cobh to join the Royal Navy on the day war broke out in 1939. Patrick served on 'HMS Furious' and 'HMS Ark Royal', amongst others. He was torpedoed twice during the war, and survived. After the war, Paddy was demobbed in Australia, where he enjoyed the remainder of his life until he died in Sydney in 1985.
**Harry Francis** also survived the war and went on to serve 35 years in the Royal Navy before retiring as Chief Petty Officer and Gunnery Instructor. He lives in Plymouth.

After a fairly inauspicious beginning in 1938 as Boy Seaman in the Mediterranean Fleet on board 'HMS Afridi', the Tribal Class Destroyer Flotilla Leader, **Larry O'Sullivan** of Ashe Street had little inkling of the hectic and hazardous events which lay in store for him during his career at sea. War clouds had gathered and Europe was plunged into the greatest conflict in the history of the world.

Destroyers took the full brunt of those early months of the war at sea. First came the Battle of the Atlantic and then the catastrophic naval campaign at Norway in 1940. After twenty-two days of continuous attacks by well-trained German aircraft, 'HMS Afridi' finally succumbed to the relentless waves of stuka dive-bombers. That was when Larry received his first introduction to the art of survival in the icy waters of the Arctic.

A few weeks later, during the evacuation of British, French and Polish forces from an area close to Dunkirk, Larry had the additional experience of being sunk by German shore batteries, fortunately in the calmer waters of the English Channel.

But it was the Battle of the Java Sea in March 1942, on board the famous cruiser 'HMS Exeter', which gave Larry his sternest test so far. This was a struggle, described by the Irish Sunday Independent as "The fiercest naval battle in history", in which the entire Allied Fleet was wiped out by the gunnery of superior Japanese warships. British, American, Dutch and Australian ships went to the bottom after a brave but futile fight to the death.

On board 'HMS Exeter' there were seven Corkmen, two of them from Youghal. When the order was given to Abandon Ship, Colman Murphy and Larry O'Sullivan sought each other out amidst the horror and chaos of those last few moments. With a loud cry of "*Moll Goggin's Corner here we come!*", the two Youghal men leaped into the warm equatorial embrace of the Java Sea. Many hours later, in the shark infested waters, the survivors were picked up and herded into slave labour camps. Here they were beaten and starved for almost four years. Of the seven Corkmen, only two came home - the Youghal pair, Murphy and O'Sullivan. Recuperation and rehabilitation from the ordeal of war and the savagery of their Japanese captors took many months.

Admiral of the Fleet, Louis the Earl Mountbatten of Burma, was to play a major role in the future career of young O'Sullivan. On his personal recommendation, Larry was hoisted from the Petty Officer's mess on board 'HMS Tyne' to the exalted status of Sub-Lieutenant RN. There was nothing particularly uplifting about a single stripe on one's sleeve, but in 1953 it was a beginning.

Following many appointments to a wide variety of naval vessels, ranging from ocean salvage tugs to submarine depot ships, Larry became a Lieutenant Commander on board the aircraft carrier 'HMS Eagle', in 1963. He also had the dubious distinction of commanding one of the last remaining coal-burning ships, 'HMS Barbican' — a far cry from the niceties of the Navy's most modern combat carrier.

Leaving warships behind, he accepted the offer of an executive position within the P&O Shipping organisation, and became principal consultant of the Marine Safety Services Division and advisor to a host of shipping companies worldwide. Tankers, cargo vessels, passenger ships, chemical and gas carriers took him to every corner of the maritime globe. It was on floor number 24 of the Standard Oil building in Chicago that he finally decided to seek the 'quiet life in a green and pleasant land'. Larry and his wife, Bridie, retired to Clonakilty in 1984.

Boy-Seaman Larry O'Sullivan
HMS Drake 1938.

Lieutenant Commander Larry O'Sullivan
HMS Eagle 1963.

The 'Jonadab' passing Ballynatray House.

The 'HMS Exeter'.
Sunk in Java Sea 2 March 1942

The 'HMS Afridi'
Sunk Norway 1940

The 'De Wadden' loading pitprops at Kilahala. *Pic: Merseyside Maritime Museum, Albert Dock, Liverpool*

# Angels of Mercy. Youghal Lifeboat Station, 1839 - 1995.

The first Youghal lifeboat was built for the Harbour Commissioners in 1839 by Taylor of Limehouse at a cost of £76.00. and was paid for by local subscription. It was stored somewhere in the Strand Street area, as the Coastguard and Custom House were originally sited at Lupton's house on the waterfront. Records show an association between the Coastguard and the Lifeboat Service at that time. The Harbour Commissioners took the decision to provide a lifeboat following a tragedy at Ferrypoint which cost the lives of twelve people.

On 2nd. February 1840, the lifeboat was called to Ardmore and towed there by horse and cart, where, under the command of Lieutenant Methrell, it rescued four people from the Brigantine 'Medora'. For this rescue, the Lieutenant was awarded the Gold Medal of the National Institution for the Preservation of Life from Shipwreck.

This was not the first medal to be won by lifesaving services in this area. In 1828, a silver medal was awarded to Lieut. Morrisson RN and then in 1836 another silver one was presented to Charles Edinton, Chief Officer of the Coastguard. In 1856, a lifeboat inspector found the lifeboat neglected in a yard, and the following year the Royal National Lifeboat Institution took over the station.

A lifeboat house was then built at a cost of £100 near Green Park, across from Poison Bush Lane and this remained in use for twenty years. A new boat was also provided and this remained on station for ten years, during which it was launched three times. One of those launches was to render help to the Barque 'Galatea' which had run aground on the bar in Youghal Bay. Fourteen lives were saved on that occasion.

In 1867, the next lifeboat, the 'William Beckett' of Leeds, arrived as a gift from that city. She and her predecessor were launched by a Boydell self-acting endless railway over the soft sand on the beach near Green Park. It was also possible to take the lifeboat on a carriage by road to launch at a place nearer to the incident. On one such occasion in 1861, when it was being brought by road to effect a rescue off Redbarn Beach, it was unsuccessful as it got stuck at the railway bridge. Later, a lifeboat helper was killed at the old boathouse, when he was jammed in the frame of the door.

Shortly after that, it was decided to move to a more suitable location. 1876 saw the present boathouse at the Mall built at a cost of £275. The 'William Beckett' of Leeds was then moved where it remained until 1885. It was launched six times and saved five lives.

The old boathouse was sold to the UDC for the storage of bathing boxes and served this purpose until demolished in 1964, when the Green Park and Lighthouse Hill were re-constructed. The 'Mary Lucombe' was the next lifeboat at Youghal Station and she remained there for 21 years. In that time, it was launched 13 times and saved 22 lives. During this period, two silver medals were awarded. In 1894 one of these was given to Harry Long, for the rescue of a young man from the yacht 'Seagull', as it foundered in Youghal Bay. Harry was grand-uncle of Jack Brookes of Pasley's Supermarket. Just recently, Miss Gile Foley of An Rinn Dungarvan, presented Harry's medal to the Youghal RNLI Station for display in their museum. The second medal was awarded in 1905 to Mike Hannigan for his part in the rescue of the schooner 'Annetta' of Dungarvan, which struck the same bar and was driven ashore near the railway station. Mike Hannigan was the grandfather of the Keogh family of Friar Street.

1906 saw the 'Mary Lucombe' replaced by the 'Marianne L. Hay', which remained on station until 1931. It was launched 15 times and saved 21 lives.

A major advance in the local Lifeboat Service took place in 1931 with the arrival of the first motor-powered lifeboat which was named the 'Laurana Sarah Blunt'. At this time also, a slipway and electric winch were installed. These replaced the rollers and slides which had to be laid down by hand. The 'Laurana Sarah Blunt' spent a rewarding 21 years here, saving 21 lives in 18 launches.

In 1952, the 'Herbert John' arrived on station, and it was with this boat that Coxwain **Richard Hickey** and crew rescued four people from the French trawler 'Fez des Ondes'. This took place at Ardmore on the 27th. October 1963, in the teeth of a south-easterly gale. Richard Hickey was awarded the Bronze medal for gallantry on that day. Also on board were **John Murphy, Michael Murphy, Christy Hennessy, Michael Hennessy, Paddy Hennessy** and **Jimmy Delaney**, all of whom received medal service certificates. The 'Herbert John' saved 30 lives during 14 launches in 14 years.

The first diesel powered boat, the 'J.B.Cooper' of Glasgow, arrived in 1966 and was replaced in 1971 by the 'Grace Darling', a Liverpool Class boat. This was launched on service 31 times to save 17 lives. An Atlantic 21 lifeboat was sent to Youghal for trials in 1983. It was the first in Ireland and was kept in the Market House for a while until the lifeboat house was adapted. This class of lifeboat introduced, for the first time, lady members to the crew. The present boat, 'Marjory Turner', also an Atlantic 21, was put on station in 1984. Since 1983, the new type of lifeboat has been on 48 service launches, resulting in 43 lives saved.

Over the past 150 years lifeboat men and women of Youghal, have rescued a total of 178 lives. Recently, further improvements have been made to the boat house, one of which was the provision of a crewroom. It was furnished from a fund set up by **Iris Shane** of Conna in memory of her husband, **Ray**, who sadly lost his life in Youghal Bay in 1985, as the result of a 'plane crash.

Another recent development was the recovery of the earliest wall-board, which gives a list of launchings, ships assisted and lives saved from 1858 to 1885. This has now been placed on the inside wall of the boat house, beside the others, and together they display a complete history. A large number of framed photographs in the crewroom help younger people to understand the tough sea conditions in which the lifeboat has to operate. It is hoped to set up a proper museum in the boat house where visitors, mariners and lifeboat enthusiasts can go for a cup of tea, while appreciating the proud history of the Youghal Lifeboat Station.

Lifeboat launch at Youghal

Maurice Hickey, Richard Hickey, David Murphy, Henry Hayes & Johnny McGrath

Richard Hickey, Commander Arbuthnot, John Murphy & Mick Murphy

# Trading Vessels.

In a Period of Years Between 1886 - 1896 vessels trading to Youghal were:

Adventure, Annie, Annie Queen, Bluebell, Bristol Packet, Brothers, Carmel, Ceres, Commerce, Dolly Varden, Eliza O'Keeffe, Elizabeth, Empire, Excel, Gypsy, Hannah, Hope, Jonadab, Lady Fielding, Lilly, Margaret, Oliver, Perth, Philanthropist, Redtail, Relief, Richard Cobden, Secret, Selena Jones, Skylark, Telephone, Thomas Annie, Thomas Edwin, Two Brothers, WHL, Wave and Wild Hunter.

Local Vessels from then onwards included:

Athena, Ariel, Asecurador, B.I., Bertha Grace, Charles, Charmaine, Citizen, Dart, Deo Gratacia, Ellen, Ellen Mar, George Peak, Jersey Tar, Kathleen and May, Mary Hounsell, Loango, Melina, Nameless, Nellie Fleming, Otacillius, Queen Victoria, Rebecca, Ring Dove, Rob Roy, Speedy, Troubador, Victor, William Edwards, William S. Green, and Wisch.

Some Irish Vessels which Traded With Youghal:

Agnes Craig, Antelope, Brooklands, Cymric, De Wadden, Ellie Park, Gaelic, Happy Harry, Harvest King, Invermore, James Postlewaite, JT&S, Mary B. Mitchell, ME Johnson, Uncle Ned, Venturer, Village Bell, William Ashbourne.

English Registered Vessels Trading with Youghal:

Alpha, Bessie Ellen, Cambourne, Donald & Doris, Earl Cairns, Elizabeth Drew, Friends, Garlandstone, Haldon, Irene, Kate, Ketch of Ayr, MA. James, Mary Miller, Maud Mary, Margaret Hobley, Millom Castle, Olive Branch, Progress, Traly, and Welcome.

The 'De Wadden' off Dunne's Park. The hull of the 'James Postlewaite' is in foreground.

*Pic: Henry Clobessy*

# Lucky Jim Cronin.

Whatever about a cat having nine lives, the late Jim Cronin of Golf Links Road and the Electricity Supply Board had at least three. In his days at sea, from 1938 to 1946, he survived bombs, torpedoes, and sinkings against all the odds. After one such miraculous escape he promised that if he managed to outlive the war, he would go to daily mass for the remainder of his life. Jim survived and kept his promise.

In 1910, Jim Cronin was born near Buttevant in North Cork. He had great hunger for learning and mastered an understanding of electricity to such a degree that he became involved in the electrification of Buttevant, Kanturk, Doneraile, Charleville and Castletownroche. They were all run by private companies then, later to be taken over by the ESB.

By 1937, Jim could not be contained in Ireland. He wanted more challenge and applied to the Blue Star Line for a position. His first posting was ashore in Liverpool as Second Electrician, servicing the ships at dockside. Then in November 1937, came his first job afloat, on the 'MV Aba' voyaging to Africa. Just two months later, he moved to the 'MV David Livingstone', on which he spent a year, again doing the African trips.

Three months on the 'SS Avelon Star' (twice to Brazil and back) brought him to September 1939, and the start of the Second World War. He was to see a lot of that war in the next few years. In Southampton, he fitted out electrically the 'Dunedin Star' from stem to stern. This ship was then put on the Australian run, during which she would hug the coast to avoid submarines. Having completed two of those long voyages, Jim was doing a job for the company on shore, when the ship left without him for its third trip. Luck was beginning to show on his side because while negotiating the Skeleton Coast she went onto a reef and stuck there. The crew managed to get ashore using the lifeboats but found themselves surrounded by miles of desert sands. During the six months that they survived in that barren place, food and water had to be dropped to them by parachute.

May 1940 saw him assigned to a cruise liner called the 'Arandora Star'. In peacetime she was well known at the best ports around the world as a ship of luxury, and was the pride of the Blue Star Line. Now she was on war service. The seaman's pass normally shows the port of departure and of arrival, plus details of the particular voyage, but from here until the end of the war, Jim's pass gave no details of the trips except to state OHMS. This meant that he was now a member of the Royal Merchant Navy.

Only two such entries in his seaman's pass mention the "arandoro star' Star' because on the second voyage she was sent to the bottom of the Atlantic by a submarine. This was one of the saddest and most controversial sinkings of the whole campaign.

When war was declared, a sizeable number of German people were already resident in Britain. In many cases they had been there for years, but now they suddenly found themselves classed as aliens. The wartime Government in Britain did not want them around in case they would somehow get intelligence messages back to their own country. Italians in Britain found themselves in the same situation. It was feared that they would take notice of ship movements, troop movements, bomb damage or even merely the morale of the people. They were not to be given the opportunity. It was decided and arranged to transport thousands of 'aliens', together with some prisoners of war, to Canada for the duration. Many were disappointed at this treatment by their adopted country but others took a different view and saw it as a way to avoid the bombings and hostilities in Europe.

The "arandoro star' Star' was chosen to carry sixteen hundred of these people, one hundred guards and another one hundred crew to Canada, making eighteen hundred aboard the ship. Normally, on her cruises, she would only carry 450 plus crew. As well as from the overcrowded conditions, the ship had been transformed to resemble a prison with miles of barbed wire used to cordon off areas. This was very dangerous as it restricted access to the rail and the lifeboats. Captain Moulton, Master of the vessel, complained about the state of the ship and the risk to transportees, guards and crew. It is said that a fraction of the wire was removed but, as events were soon to reveal, it was not enough.

Ship's electrician, **Jim Cronin**, was as anxious as everybody else when they sailed from Liverpool with their human cargo on June 29th. 1940 to cross the Atlantic. Unknown to them, German submarine U-47, under the command of Captain Gunther Prien, was heading for home, having already sunk 9 steamships. U-47 had only one *'bugato'* (torpedo) left for its journey back to base. It was to be one too many.

Early on the morning of July 2nd., the "arandoro star' Star' crossed paths with the submarine. Captain Prien had no notion of what cargo was being carried on the ship, as he lined it up in his sights. The single torpedo was aimed at the engine room of the secret floating prison. Jim Cronin was due to start his shift in the engine room at 7a.m. and a thoughtful steward arrived with a timely cup of hot tea. Those few moments sipping the tea saved his life. As he handed back the cup, the ship was rocked by an explosion so severe that it needed no explanation. He knew it had to be a torpedo strike. Grabbing his life-jacket he dashed into the corridor. The doors of the engine room had been blown off their hinges and lay in the alleyway. A strong smell of cordite confirmed his worst fears. Two of his fellow engineers and two greasers were drowned by the water that poured in to flood the turbines and generators. As Jim advised his remaining mates to head for open deck, Captain Moulton gave the order to abandon ship. Guards and internees tore at the barbed wire with their guns and bare hands. Some managed to escape from the terrible catastrophe. Of 1,800 on board only 800 were saved, including the ever lucky Jim Cronin.

Malta was the scene for his next close shave and this time it was even more dangerous. The battle for the island was a drawn-out ferocious one. Tunnels honeycombed its rocky structure and it was in these that the defenders and populace sought refuge from the prolonged saturation bombings that seemed out of all proportion to the size of the place. The islanders gave stubborn resistance, but they needed to be supplied. This was when the Blue Star Line ships, and others, ran their most terrible risks.

December 1941 saw a convoy of supply ships with escorts take an awful hammering from air attack as they made their way to port in Valetta, to be received to the great cheers of the Maltese. The 'Empire Star', with Jim Cronin aboard, was one of that famous convoy. But if getting in was tough, what about the going home? Christmas was just a few days away and the strategists made ready to sail out, under cover of darkness, on December 24th., in the hope that the festivities would distract their attackers.

Just after dark on Christmas Eve, the remaining ships (some had been sunk on the way in) made their way quietly out of the harbour into the Mediterranean. It went well for a time and their confidence was growing as they got further away from the island. But then, as if somebody flicked a switch, the whole scene exploded as torpedoes hit home, one after the other, like regulated fireworks. What had been an eerie sea of shadows heading for home now became bright as day from the torchlight of vessels, in their last agony. Jim, on the 'Empire Star', was deep in the engine room with a mate of his and they busied themselves, trying to ignore the commotion in the sea around them. They realised that their luck could not last and, sure enough, a torpedo came clean through the side of the vessel, just above the water line, and exited through the other side, without exploding. In doing so, however, it hit the mate, carrying the top half of his body away. A small pile of bloody flesh and bone was all that remained where Jim's friend had stood seconds before.

A short time after his fright at Malta, Jim was on the 'Sydney Star' as she steamed near Gibraltar in convoy with 23 other vessels. They were savagely attacked and the devastation was so concentrated that only 4 ships survived the onslaught. Needless to say the 'Sydney Star' with Jim on board was one of these.

In 1944, he joined the 'Australian Star' and his position was then Chief Electrician. He remained with this ship until his retirement from the sea in 1946. Jim returned to Mallow to work for the E.S.B. and in 1948 he transferred to Youghal. He married Nora Dorgan, a nurse from his home area, whom he had met in England.The ceremony was performed by an old friend of his, Father Tom Paul Geary.

In later years Jim's survival training came to the fore when he was involved in the rescue of a young boy at the quayside. While sauntering along Nealon's Quay (Burnt Stores), Danny Hurley saw a red object floating in the current about twenty yards out. He peered intently and realized that it was a child floating face down in the water. Without hesitation,

Danny jumped in and bore the lifeless boy ashore. The child was four year old Kevin Cooney of the Mall. Jim Cronin saw the excitement, and went to help. His knowledge of resuscitation methods were put to good use and he knew exactly what to do, stuck well to the task and managed to revive the boy.

In his retirement, he kept in touch with old friends all over Europe. He once said "You make many friends on sinking ships". It took the old age of seventy-seven years to sink Jim Cronin in May of 1987.

Lucky Jim Cronin

# Flashing Light.

Mention the word lighthouse and people think of near-inaccessible places like rock-projections, foam-washed headlands and isolated islands. But here and there can be found exceptions and the Youghal lighthouse is one. No isolation, no rationing, and no dashing through spray from dwelling house to tower. To walk out the front door in Youghal, onto the footpath leading into town, is to enter a civilian world so different to a conventional Keeper's life. One Lightkeeper, who had served on Tory Island, Rathlin Island, Roches Point, Hook Head and Tuskar Rock, before his final appointment to Youghal, told of the culture shock on arrival here.

On the first day, when he walked out 'on-top' to the rail, he was overwhelmed by the noise from the traffic on the busy N25 Cork to Rosslare road  behind him. "To me," he said, "it was like being landed in the middle of New York City". Local people pass by this famous landmark without a second glance. It takes visitors to notice the contrast and beauty of what is a perfectly functional lighthouse, located in the middle of an urban district. With the Strand and Summerfield areas rapidly becoming built up, the town is spreading out more and more beyond the famous Lighthouse Hill.

Next to the boundary wall, a pedestrian path leads down to the rocky outcrops at sea level. This walkway is said to be the oldest passageway in town and is still in use. Even before the town's existence, it was used by all kinds of mariners. Friends of the area like fishermen and merchants, foes like invaders and pirates have all stepped up that steep climb.

The first lighthouse was erected by the Normans in the 12th. century on the same location as the present one. A convent was also built beside the tower so that the nuns could conveniently tend to the light. The clever Normans knew that the nuns would be most dependable and would have the respect and support of the natives, thereby ensuring a reliable light.

This early tower was just thirty feet high and had two windows, facing east and south. The windows face the same directions to indicate the channels in the bar across the bay. The fire was lit at window level in wet weather and on the roof when fine. It was a tribute to those first Norman tower engineers that the present lighthouse was built 700 years later in roughly the same position.

For 300 years, from the mid-16th century, the coastal warning lights were removed. Many pirates and plunderers had imitated the fires in the wrong places, and so ships had been lured to disaster on the rocky shores where they were looted.

In 1848, it was decided to replace the 'Lights' at some points on the south coast. At first it was thought that one should be put on Capel Island, but would be of little help to vessels entering Youghal Harbour. The building of the present tower commenced in 1848, near the site of the old convent, and its light first shone over the bay in February of 1852.

Granite is the stone of the red-railinged white tower and it rises 45 feet over three floors with the water mark 80 feet below. In the mid-sixties, the light was converted to electricity thereby increasing the power. Nowadays it uses a single 100v., 1000w., BSL11 lamp and flashes every 2.5 seconds. It can be seen 18 nautical miles away, which is almost 21 statute miles.

The present Keeper of the Light still goes through the

same type of day as he did on Skellig Michael off the Kerry coast, many years ago. He studies the weather, the tides and the currents as he watches over the fishing boats, pleasure craft and cargo vessels. Even on calm days, there are still maintenance jobs to be done.

The sight of a lighthouse always brings a sense of security to sailors, active or retired. One old tar said that he would only live on shore if within sight of a lighthouse. Then at night, he explained, the flashing light would break the darkness on his window pane and he would sleep soundly as if safe at anchor.

Youghal Lighthouse

# Shipping Movements
## Youghal February 1939

4th. Schooner 'Cymric' sailed, having discharged 325 tons coal for Youghal Gas Works,- Hall, Master.

8th. Schooner 'Happy Harry' sailed from upriver with timber,- Hagan, Master.

12th. Ketch 'Bessie Ellen' arrived with coal for upriver,- Lamey, Master.

13th. Steamship 'Kyle Skye' arrived with 253 tons coal for M.J.Fleming ,- Brines, Master.

15th Steamship 'Kyle Skye' sailed light. Schooner 'Haldon' arrived windbound,- W.Slade, Master. Schooner 'Haldon' sailed after windbound.

18th. Schooner 'Margaret Hobley' arrived windbound, – J.Slade, Master. Ketch 'C. F. H.' arrived windbound, – Stribling, Master.

19th. Schooner 'Happy Harry' arrived with coal for upriver. Steamship 'Kyle Skye' arrived with 260 tons coal for M.J.Fleming.

21st. Steamship 'Kyle Skye' sailed light.

22nd. Schooner 'Margaret Hobley' sailed after windbound.

27th. Ketch 'C. F. H.'. sailed after windbound.

# Queen Victoria's Visit to Queenstown.

Local Youghal mariners were not anxious to take their craft to Queenstown (Cobh) as part of the flotilla of honour for the visiting Queen Victoria in 1849. This was just after the Great Hunger of 1845-47. The general population was still suffering from lack of energy and depression and in no mood to celebrate anything.

Shipowners in town were anxious that Youghal be represented somehow and so they decided to take the yacht 'Arub' to Queenstown themselves. It was to be a very memorable adventure for all the wrong reasons. As they left Youghal harbour they crashed into a schooner. Then, as they entered Cork Harbour, the yacht caught fire which was quickly extinguished. Next they rammed and sunk another craft before taking their place in the procession, very close to the Royal Yacht.

And to crown their sorrows, the flag bearing the arms of Youghal got caught in the rigging and could not be dipped. There was much criticism from nautical circles in Queenstown for many years afterwards.

Preparing the nets under the 'masts' while Moby Dick was being filmed in Youghal.
Pictured are Johnny & Bunny Buttimer. Pic: Michael McKeown

Mikie Ronayne, Bob Webster & Jimo O'Donoghue mending their nets

# Drift-net Fishing.

When drift-net fishermen go out on the water to fish, they 'pay out' their nets at 'berths', which are marks taken from the shoreline, just as their forefathers did. From Old Strancally Castle, six miles upriver, to Pilmore, at the far side of Youghal Bay, the berths are used like invisible name signs.

Just as road markings show the plan of a road, so too, the berths are the plan of a fishing river. There is honour between fishermen and if a berth is taken (in use), the next comer goes to a different one. The names they are known by can be related to landmarks on the shore, events of long ago in that place, or the formation of the riverbed. The Irish names are very old and , as in the case of *Líne na Sagart*, historical. In that name, the purge of monasteries and abbeys is recalled from the time when soldiers were sent to sack Molana Abbey (Dair-Inis), just north of Templemichael Castle. The monks in the Abbey took flight using a line of small boats, trying desperately to escape. Sadly, however, all the boats were sunk, and the monks were drowned. Ever since, that part of the river, including the fishing berth, has been known as *Líne na Sagart*, or in English, The Line of the Priests.

Starting near Clashmore, the berths are: The Bank - Ballinaclash; Líne- na-Sagart, The Abbey Hole (riverbed depression near Dair-Inis), The Ferry (old ferry crossing from Ardsallagh to Temple-Michael), The Pond, The Beannacht (the Blessing), The Cuilín (the Small Bay), The Bearna (the Gap), Bridge Hole (riverbed depression near old bridge), Bog of Allen (mudflats at mouth of Tourig tributary). We then reach the site of the old Youghal Metal Bridge.

Moving on downriver - Slobín or The Step (small

marsh); Cuilín-Glen (small bay glen);.Trágh (strand); Power's (upper berth); The Barracks (lower berth); Kennedy's (Bunny Buttimer always called this one The Garden Gate); The Bush; Church (old church ruin); The Angle (by the gap); Aerial.

That brings us to the Ferrypoint. Swinging in the Cool (refers to swinging with the strong current); The Corner; The Stake. Over at the Cork side of the river – Cannister Way (off the slob-bank corner and Bridge Angle (buttress on Cork side of metal bridge).

In olden fishing times, when yawls were more numerous on the river, a section of harbour-mouth from the Green Park wall to Susan Hurley's Esplanade Hotel on the seafront was considered out of bounds. It was called the 'Resting Place' and was intended to give the salmon untroubled breathing space following their crossing of the Atlantic. After such a rest, the fish would swim strongly upriver, ready to overcome obstacles like rapids, waterfalls and weirs – if not nets.

Westwards from the Head of the Rock (Moll Goggin's) corner, The Bounds, The Groyne, Strand Gap, Muiríoch, Corduroys, Coolbhán (White bay), Stacks Stones (large stones, now buried by sands), Parcín Joachim (Joachim's field), Ceann an Bhóthair (Head of the Road), Neill's Ligs, Neill's Slip, Flavin's Slip, The Geata (the gate), Cliann Isteach (term used when a man marries into a farm), Philly's Boreen, The Stat (the state), The Port, Cuinnegar (projection at Pilmore, also known as The Barrels).

An interesting feature of fishing from Ceann an Bhóthair (Redbarn), was that yawls had to be rolled down the beach on timbers to the water. The boats were large and heavy and took tough handling to launch. The Barony men (from that area) would have to endure the same hardship, having fished the tide, to bring their boats back above the high water line on the strand.

This was in harsh contrast to the town fishermen who could enter a dock and moor to a bollard without any trouble. Another difference was that when the salmon were running at Ceann an Bhóthair, a donkey cart would be brought down to meet the boat and take the fish from it. Hardships experienced by the fishermen of Ceann an Bhóthair were also endured by the Monatrea fishermen, as a result of not having a quay on their own side of the river.

The following warning has been sent, in jest, to the families and friends of some Youghal sailors returning from long sea trips:

*"Fill the fridge with beer. Get his best clothes out of the mothballs/pawnshop. Ensure local girlfriends are made aware of his imminent arrival. Very soon your sailor will be in your midst again, somewhat dehydrated, a trifle radio-active, and much demoralised. In making your joyous preparations to welcome him back to civilisation, you should make allowance for the rather crude environment which has been his unfortunate lot for the past months/years. Show no sign of alarm if he prefers to sit cross-legged on the floor, wearing nothing but a towel. He will probably scream at the least sign of a banana or coconut. Do all his shopping for him and try to reassure him that all bartering, haggling, cajoling or threatening of shopkeepers is no longer necessary, now that he is back in the Youghal area.*

*His language may be a trifle embarrassing at first but in a fairly short time he can be made to speak properly again. Finally, treat him with kindness, tolerance and regular quarts of bearable brandy and you will be quite surprised how readily he accepts you."*

Jack Griffin, Jimmy Hogan, Tom Joe O'Keeffe, Frank Owens, Jim Hurley & Dick White.
*Pic Michael McKeown*

**Blessing the fishing boats at Market Quay in the 1930s.** *Pic: Horgans*

A story-telling session in Paddy Linehan's pub 1954 *Pic Michael McKeown*

Quayside chat. Willie Lynch, Florrie Coakley, Jim Healy & Jimmy Mulcahy. *Pic: Michael McKeown*

On the occasion of the landing of a 46 lb salmon

Willie Sparoway, Paddy Coakley (with child), Tommy O'Mahony & Jimmy Mulcahy

# A Look Back in Time at Cork Hill.

It's remarkable how times have so changed to make all the inhabitants of the town lock and bolt their doors at night. It is very different from not too long ago when doors were left open twenty- four hours a day. Babies were born at home and, at the other end of life,the elderly and ill were kept with their families to the end. Neighbours were a supportive presence popping in and out at any opportunity.

**Lizzie Twomey** of Lower Cork Hill never locked her door and on fine Summer nights not only would it be unlocked, but it could be wide ajar, back to the wall. She told the story herself of waking early on a fairday morning to a loud commotion downstairs. Tiptoeing to the landing, she saw two farmers sitting on the bottom steps of her stairway, discussing the price of the six sheep in her hall.

**Willie Lyons** reminded me that a person was considered a true Londoner if he lived within hearing distance of the famous Bow Bells. At home in Youghal, a real Cork-Laner was one who lived within hearing distance of the Cork-Hill Pipe Band practice hall.

**Paidín Kiely** was another Cork Hill dweller and he had a donkey and cart to help him to make his living. While downtown one day, he left his donkey and cart tied at the pole outside his house. The local lads decided to play a trick on him and quickly untackled the donkey and dismantled the cart. Then, bringing the whole lot into Paidín's kitchen, they promptly made it all up perfectly again. They barely had time to hide behind the wall across the road before he arrived back up at the house. Paidín immediately missed the donkey and cart, and walked around the road for a few minutes, scratching his head, wondering where he had left them. Concealed across the way, the boys were trying to stifle their laughter, and with them was his own son, **Larry**, enjoying it all. In a bothered state, Paidín decided to make a cup of tea before starting to look for the missing animal. What a shock he got! The donkey and cart, ready for the road, was in the kitchen. But he was a clever gent and guessed correctly at the first attempt. Running out into the road, he started to shout out all the names of the lads in the area. Then the laughter poured forth over the wall. They could not keep it in any longer. "I know ye", said Paidín, "ye've gone too far, I'm going down for the Guards", and off he went.

Quickly and expertly the lot was taken apart in the kitchen and remade again, outside the house, by the laughing youngsters. Hardly had they finished and were back inside the wall, when they spied Paidin approaching with two large Gardaí. He was walking between them, nodding and shaking his head, in an effort to get them to believe what had happened. But of course, as they rounded the bend, by Jack Daly's shop, there was the donkey and cart tied nice and neatly to the pole outside the house. Paidín had a red face as he listened to more laughter from over the wall.

On a more serious note, one mother with a young family was so poor, that when her children arrived home from school looking for something to eat, she would pretend to be cooking the dinner. Not a scrap of food would be in the house and all would depend on her fisherman husband catching a few fish. Pending his return, she would point to the pot over the fire and tell the children that the potatoes were not cooked yet. They would all glance into the pot wishfully before jumping out to play in the lane, believing their mother. What they did not know was that in the pot the mother had nice-sized round stones resembling potatoes and so she managed to keep the truth from the children. Later, if her husband arrived with a fish plus a few bob, dinner went ahead.

Daly's shop, halfway up Cork Hill, was an institution. **Anna** and **Jack Daly** stood behind the counter of their small premises with its loft bedroom overhead. Larry would give a hand when home on holidays and a neighbour, **Peggy Daly**, helped there for years. The handmade bread, loose milk and vegetables with fresh clay still on them, are remembered. Jack also worked the family farm behind Kenny's Lane, across the road, with the help of **Paddy Fitzgerald** and **Sam Riordan**. Like all small shops that time, most customers got credit until payday when the whole weeks groceries would be paid for together. "Put it on the book" was all a child had to say. A lot of poor people with big families found it hard to manage and often could not meet their weekly settlement, but they were still given more food 'on the book'.

**Larry Daly** was great fun and always good for a laugh. An old black bicycle was his transport and was all that he wanted. His casual relaxed appearance on that machine belied his academic qualifications and his command of six languages. This was very evident one day at Farrell's shop when a French tourist wanted directions to Mount Mellary. She could only speak French and was having difficulty getting help, until Larry arrived on his bike. Recognising her dilemma and accent, he addressed her in excellent French. Her mouth fell open in wonder at the talent of this unassuming cyclist, as he proceeded to give instructions perfectly, in her own tongue.

A fish coddle, in a pot on the crane over the fire, was a cosy, warm assurance in any house in the 1920s. Halfway up Cork Hill lived a kind old woman on her own and she encouraged poor children to call on her after school. She liked their company and would help with their homework before giving them a bowl of coddle. She adored them and they loved her. Years later, in far off lands, those people thought back to their childhood and the nice old woman. Only then did they realise that helping with their lessons was just a ploy to enable her to feed poor hungry children.

Larry Kiely, Cork Hill.

Noel Purcell sings with Mick Delahunty & his Orchestra at the Showboat

*Pic: Michael McKeown*

John McGrath 1994 atop the Clock Gate overlooking the town. He lived there with his parents until 1959. *Pic: Denis Scannell, Cork Examiner*

# Tallow Street in the 1950s.

Two big old pennies each was our 'pay' every Friday night when my father came home from the Post-Office with his wages. He was a night telephonist in those years and, as he would be in bed on Saturday (his pay-day), after a night's work, he alone got paid on Friday evening. Those two pennies meant so much to us. What value we could get as we rushed off to the sweet shop windows to behold the boxes of offerings on display.

**Tommy Flavin's** and **Mary Murphy's** were our two nearest shops in Tallow St., but on Friday night we went to the sweets-only shops. **Cashell's**, next to Pender's Lane at 161 North Main St. (where **Ned Coyne** later had his butcher shop) and **Mrs. Roche's** (next to **Jim Parker's**), were like magnets to children with pennies to spend. Hidden forces drew us to view magnificent arrays of sweets and penny bars.

The dilemma was would it be Tasty Value or Lasting Value. Usually we went for the Lasting Value like hard-boiled sweets, clove rocks or squares of solid slab toffee. No wonder local dentist **Frank Ferguson** had a massive job to do on my teeth when I was just fourteen. And Mrs Kitty Cashell – oh, how her patience was tried around 7p.m. every Friday night as we banged on the solid timber counter for service! She would appear from the back kitchen without a murmur of protest, even though she could be at her tea or listening to 'The Archers' on the B.B.C.at the time.

Having purchased our goodies, we would amble home, chewing all the way. Public lighting was scarce and of poor quality then with a lamp only every third pole, but the lights from the shop windows lit up the footpaths for us. As

Christmas would approach, my mother would encourage us to get a moneybox and save up for Santa. "Maybe," she would say "one of your pennies could be saved every week ?" We agreed. But next Friday was a long way off to stick to such a resolution. Anyway a cardboard box wouldn't have a hope of lasting our 'low' days. If saving was to be done, then a proper tin money-box would have to be got.

There was a lovely Royal Mail type letter-box in the toy shop and I asked Santa to bring me one – until my mother found out. "What good is a money box on Christmas morning?", she asked. I had to agree. Eventually I did manage to buy the tin money box and was convinced that saved coins were unrecoverable until the box would fill so much as to blow the lid off. Its ability to perform that questionable trick was never tested. The narrow slit, through which the pennies were pushed, was said to be too narrow for a knife plus penny to fit together. Wrong! We had very thin-worn knives that my father had brought from his people in Mill Road, when he got married. If things went right, a penny could be flicked out of the box in about five seconds. It did give us the 'security' of having a few pennies as a kind of cushion for 'emergencies' but it never got to more than a few. Amusing to think that all those brainy people who invented trains and tracks, walkie-talkie dolls and cap-gun revolvers could not produce a child-proof money box.

Entering Youghal from the Waterford direction in the 1950s, the first shop encountered was the Variety Stores in Tallow Street. Two quiet sisters, Miss Costelloe and Mrs. Coleman, sold all kinds of ware, cutlery, small hardware, religious goods, and, at Christmas time, toys. Our only interest in the shop suddenly awakened every November when the big plate-glass window was dressed with all the toys and trimmings of the season. Mrs. Coleman would give the outside of the glass a special cleaning for the switch-on of the window fairylights. Then we would appear in force to ogle at the large selection of cowboy guns, trains and tracks, dolls, cars, jigsaws and games. At first we would just stare, letting all the colours and lights whisk us away to fantasyland. But then some boy would shout "I bags that train!". What he meant was that he was 'booking' it and nobody else dare buy it. (Nobody thought that the shop could have more than one of the same item). And so the game went on, until all the best toys were 'bagged'. After a while we tried to see more of the toys by pressing close to the window at an angle, dirty noses all over the polished surface. "Get away from the window!", the soft shout would ring out and we would all run around the corner to hide. The lady would then give the glass a fresh polish but two minutes later we would sneak back quietly, wet noses again to the window. "Look over here!", some boy would say and snotty noses would make trails like snails across the shining plate glass. "Get away!" How those two women earned the sale of their toys.

**Johnny Walsh** lived at No. 4 Tallow St. in a small terraced house with an attic loft where he kept his store of odds and ends. Johnny was a very happy man, full of life, who had spent his younger years in showbusiness. He had toured with circuses like Corvenios and Lintons. Juggling, magic, clowning and tap dancing all came easily to him and even in later life he organised and took part in variety concerts at the Town Hall on the Mall. Fred Astaire would have approved of Johnny's clear loud dance steps on the boards of that Mall House stage.

The secret was that his friend Johnny McCarthy, the Blacksmith, put heavy donkey tips on the dance shoes. Johnny Walsh earned his living in many ways, as a bill-poster, furniture remover and auctioneer's assistant. For years he had ridden a tricycle with a large timber box in front to bring all his posters, brushes and paste. Later he purchased a motorised version and would purr around town proudly on that unusual vehicle. Johnny was a well-known member of Youghal society in the 1940s and 50s.

Johnny Walsh *Pic Ml. Roche*

Johnny McCarthy at his forge

**Joe Hallissey** of Ashe Street (right) was a popular photographer in Youghal. He was also known as a motor mechanic, electrician, journalist, publisher, historian, actor, magician and as a man who did a lot for his town. In 1949.he published 'A History & Guide to Youghal'

# The Ropewalk.

Towards the end of the last century, in the shadow of Youghal's famous Town Walls, a most unusual trade was carried on by the **O'Sullivan** family of Ashe Street. It was rope making and the Ropewalk occupied the strip of land which meandered along the base of the historical walls, on the western side of the town. Ships needed ropes, and the 56,000 British troops garrisoned in Ireland depended on the lively shipping communications across the Irish Sea, thus ensuring an energetic ropemaking industry which augured well for the O'Sullivan family in the seaport town of Youghal

In the beginning the Ropewalk had three parallel levels, each approximately 300 yards in length and well able to accommodate the 120 fathom (240 yards) berthing hawsers for the ships in the bustling harbour. Alas, by 1920, only one operational level remained, carefully controlled and strictly supervised by old John O'Sullivan of Ashe Street.

There was no Raheen Park in those years and even Sarsfield Terrace (built in 1936) was not yet in existence. So from Aher's Terrace (Town Walls) to the perimeter of the old Fever Hospital, was a junctionless stretch of narrow road beside which the O'Sullivans conducted their craft. Browne's drays and railway horses would collect the huge bales of hemp, jute and sisal at the Youghal Railway Station for delivery to the Ropewalk where teams of men and mules transformed the raw materials to meet the needs of a wide variety of customers.

Apart from ships' requirements,there were twines and lines for the flourishing fishing fleet; soft-laid short spancils for the fetlocks of farmers' horses to prevent the animals from roaming too far; and there were balls of string for shops to secure purchases. **Keane's Hardware** and **Irish Mike's**, near the Clock Gate, displayed and distributed the finished products and O'Sullivans ropes found their way onto the decks of ships and the bollards of distant seaports for three generations.

But the new technology of mass production overtook the Youghal Ropewalk. O'Sullivan's Ropes faded into the past, having written an honourable paragraph in a page of Youghal's history.

The restored town walls towering over the Ropewalk.
*Pic: Billy Collins*

# A Quick Intake.

Sir Joseph McKenna of Ardo, Ardmore, was the last member of Parliament to represent the Youghal area. Tyntes Castle at 148 North Main Street was built by the Walsh family in 1602 and leased to Sir Richard Tynte. He is buried in Kilcredan cemetery near Ballymacoda.

Where the Post-Office is now situated, used to stand a fine period townhouse, fronted by wrought-iron railings, and called the White House. It was owned by the Farrell family. In the early part of this century, Farrell's installed an electricity generator in their yard at Catherine St. to power their town properties.

The Red House, White House plus nearby grocer's shop, the meal and paint store (across from Alms Houses) and the corn stores near the double slips were all powered by Farrells' generator. At this time, the rest of the town had none and so the Farrells offered to wire and connect the whole town to the system. **Jack Tooher**, whose wife later had the St. Annes Nursing Home, was the expert who had performed the electrical work on the Farrell properties and was now ready to wire the town. But the offer was declined by the UDC as it was felt that any such venture would be harmful to their own local Gas Works.

Cross Lane is so called because until the middle of the 16th century, a large Norman Cross stood in the middle of the street at that junction.

Keane's shop at 100-101 North Main Street (now Cal Flavins) was, at one time, a boot factory employing many shoemakers and cobblers. The factory was later purchased by Merricks and so all the plant was moved across the road, where it functioned for several more years.

O'Rahilly Street (ESB) was previously called Nile Street after Nelson's victory at the battle of the Nile.

Where the Fish-Co-op. is now located, on the approach to the Pier Head, was the Fish Market of the last century.

The large carpark behind the new fire station is where the 'Burnt Stores' stood for years. Those tall roofless walls served as yards and even slaughter houses for butchers until they were demolished for safety reasons. Originally the stores housed tons of butter and other produce ready for export to all parts. Then one night, a fire started and it quickly spread to set the butter alight. So intense was the heat, that the flaming butter flowed like lava from the windows onto the water to make a river of fire.

The Mall House, or Town Hall as it is now known, was built as a town house for the Duke of Devonshire. A daughter of the Earl of Cork had married the fourth Duke.

Mayor Stout was the last Mayor of Youghal and the position ceased in 1840.

Where the Loreto Convent now stands was at an earlier time owned by Lucinda Louisa Hyde, aunt of Dr. Douglas Hyde, the first President of Ireland.

The present main road to Cork, via Summerfield, was built in 1810. Before that the way to Cork was via Cork Hill and on by the Old Killeagh Road.

*(From the tapes of Bobby Chapel, courtesy of Noel Cronin).*

Paddy Fitzgerald & son John ploughing high over the town at Windmill Hill. *Pic: Bob Rock*

# A Treasury of Memories.

The rich sea and river harvest around Youghal meant plenty of fresh fish available to be distributed in town and country. "Fish Joulters" was what the sellers were called as they went about disposing of their spratt, mackerel, whiting, pollock and cod. **Jack Rapley**, in his small grey van, was one of the salesmen who travelled the countryside. **Chrissie**, his wife, was always beside him on his journeys and they always seemed happy calling from house to house.

Jack could be very evasive when replying to inquisitive people . As was said long ago, 'he could act the cute fool'. He was stopped by a Garda in Tallow and asked "*Have you this one insured?*". The Garda meant the van but Jack reacted as if Chrissie was the subject. "*I have*" said Jack, "*a shilling and sixpence a week with Joe Aherne, the insurance man*". All the Garda could do was open his mouth, close his eyes and guffaw loudly. When he opened his eyes, Jack was gone.

Another story, again concerning Tallow, tells of Jack calling to the Parish Priest's house on a Friday morning, hoping to make the sale of a fish. But during those war years of the 1940s, unknown to Jack, the laws on fasting and abstinence were rescinded in the diocese of Waterford and Lismore. Jack was therefore surprised when the Parish Priest's housekeeper refused to buy any fish from him. He was doubly shocked when he got the smell of steak from the kitchen. "Come on," he said to Chrissie, "we'll sell no fish in this town today, even the Parish Priest is having a steak for his dinner".

Clothes and food were the two big expenses when we were growing up. People had no cars, and so had no tax and insurance bills. Likewise there were no telephones, televisions, or electrical gadgets – just the electric light.

Gas was used for cooking and was paid for gradually as the meter swallowed the pennies. Then **Leo Whelan** came to clear it and give us back the surplus. Families had an account book in at least one nearby grocery shop where a week's credit was given. Sometimes heated words would be exchanged at reckoning hour when a customer would question the total to be settled. This could be the result of some oversmart kids getting things 'on the book' without parental knowledge or it could be a case of a busy shopkeeper reaching for the wrong book. At times, customers insisted on having a second book of their own to keep track of the goods bought. However, payday saw it all straightened out, ready for another week's credit. Willie Neville's Drapery shop carried a great number of accounts 'on the book' and whatever the occasion, any garment in the place could be brought home on approval without fee. Even as many as six coats could be held overnight for a kind of home fashion show. The chosen garment would be kept and the others returned the next morning, all for a regular half-crown per week (or five shillings as the family grew up). It seems that there was no end to the amount of bad debts that were carried by those shops as a secret gesture to poor people.

An old man told me that when he was a boy, a snooty insensitive mother could not resist coming down the laneway calling her 'Dotey Pet' for his tea. "Come on pet, your sausages and two eggs are ready !", she would shout. All the other boys would stop playing as if stung. They knew very well that no sausages or eggs awaited the rest of them at home. Just bread and jam if they were lucky. If not, bread and dripping. As a woman said "Dip in the dip and let the herrin' to your father".

The wife of any salmon fisherman endured a perpetual state of anxiety as they lived on a day-to-day basis. In bad weather, her husband risked his life so that they could eat and then in worse weather, when the gales blew and the boats could not go out, the fish coddle had to keep them going. Our elders remember when the wives of the fishermen would go down to the quayside to wave to their menfolk out on the water. But there was another reason for this. If the fish were running (being caught), the husband would raise his hands to show how many salmon were in the boat and the happy wife would head for the grocery shop to buy food for dinner. That was a good day. On a bad day, when no hand was held up, the woman returned home to stir her pot of yesterday's coddle.

**Michael Ruane** of Clifton, at 96 years of age, is the only survivor of the local Gardaí of the 1950s. **Sergeants Alec O'Beirne** and **William Lupton, Gardaí Nicholas Caesar, Tom Carroll, Joe Dempsey, Matt Fottrell, Michael Griffin, John Stack** and **Denis Windle** were his comrades in that era. Times were different then. Crime was mainly petty, and pub closing time, dogs without licenses and unlit bikes at night were keenly watched. A great story, attributed to Guard Caesar, says it all. A youth was noticed stealing chocolate from a shop in Friar Street and Guard Caesar, who lived around the corner at Water Street, was sent for. He collared the youth and brought him to the Barracks near the quayside to give him a good talking-to. The aim was to encourage him to resist temptation. Guard Caesar soon realised that this youth had nobody to advise him at home and could be hungry as well. With this in mind he gave the boy a sixpence to go and buy biscuits for them, while he put on the kettle. The young lad appreciated the goodwill of the kind elderly man and went willingly to the shop, over-anxious to please. Five minutes later, he returned with a big smile. "There are your biscuits, Sir, and that's your sixpence back."

In the 1920s, when boys wanted hurleys to play with, they walked out to the countryside to seek a piece of ash from some farmer. A small entire root or a piece from a big one was their objective. Strong *buachaillí* would borrow a cross-cut saw to cut up a root of ash too big to bring away and if some lad had a bike, it could bring the weight of the timber along the road. Failing that, the ash would be deposited by the roadside until a donkey-cart or horse-cart appeared on its way to town. Pleas from the hurlers usually won the heart of the driver, and timber and lads piled onto the cart. **Paddy Dwyer** worked the large circular saw at Tommy Murray's timber yard in Catherine Street, before Jim Parker's time, and he knew what to expect when he saw the donkey-cart arrive with its load. The boys muttered a fast "thank you" for their lift as they hauled the ash root over to Paddy at the circular-saw table.

Awkward looking planks resulted from the cutting, and because they only remotely resembled hurleys, a lot of elbow grease had to be used. Up at Donoghue's field (later to become Mrs. Murphy's garden in Tallow Street) this next stage was done. A spokeshave was procured to pare down the rough planks and so handle, shaft and boss began to appear on each one. For the final rounding-off work, glass was best, and freshly broken jam jars had just the right curve for this purpose. The finished article was a work of art, a labour of love. So with great pride and glee, the boys played hurling in Donoghue's field, back in the 1920s. North Abbey Cemetery now incorporates Donoghue's field.

# Lombard's Pub.

The Beatles pop group had a "B" side record which said "There's a place where I can go, when I feel low" and it reminds me of that lovely little country pub on the road from Youghal to Tallow, about three miles out. A visitor could be sure of a welcome by the Licensee, **Frances Casey**, in the daytime or by her husband **Mick** at night.

It was a small pub, with seating for about six on the high stools, six more on the wall seats and an extra few would fill it up. The overflow would drift into the adjoining tap-room, which was about the same size. Timber counter, timber shelves and a tiled floor took us back a hundred years to relax as our grandfathers did. During their Bowling matches, they would rest at this haven for their nourishment. That Tallow Road has always been a bowling area and many the cup was filled and a good celebration had, after a 'score'.

The pheasant shooting season brought out the fowlers and they would call in on their way home. Frances had a stuffed pheasant high on a shelf over the bottles and the gunmen could claim honestly to have seen at least one bird on their travels.

This was a place where people who worked hard on the land met in the evenings to relax and where the walkers or cyclists from town brought the news to country friends and in turn learned the price of livestock or the yield of an acre of corn. It was a good healthy mix of lifestyles. There was amusement on the country faces as the townie told of working 'late' until 7p.m., while the farm hand had no regular hours and might have to get up at night for a calving cow. From 1954, Lombards became a Post-Office as well and so became even more of a community gathering point.

Farmers would meet there, with the area rep. **Kevin Coughlan** of Ardmore, to hear of their beet acreage allocation for the year. It all shows that for any event in the south of the Knockanore Parish, Lombards was the place.

On Saturday night, January 20th. '73, my stag party was held in that country pub and it was great. But unknown to us as we sang away the hours, a terrible accident happened further up the road. A car crash claimed the lives of brothers, **Mossy and John Hannon**, as they returned from a visit to their sister **Lizzie** in Mallow. Mossy had been the Manager of the Youghal Gas Works for years and John was a well known shopkeeper in Tallow Street. My father Mick and the Hannon brothers had been reared together at Mill Road.

In the late 1940s and early 50s, there was a rule for pubs that only people who were more than three miles from home could be served on a Sunday. Lombard's was just the place for the Youghal people to walk to and earn their 'traveller' tag. The North Road would be busy every Sunday as the locals walked the distance to qualify for their pints. From Cork Hill corner to Lombard's is exactly three miles and so, strictly speaking, people living on the north side of the corner were not 'travellers'. Frances Casey turned a blind eye and everybody was welcomed equally.

One Sunday evening the Youghal contingent, as they sang and danced their way happily home, removed the big heavy iron gates from Blida House for a bit of fun. The next morning, the owner, **Mr. O'Gorman**, discovered the blackguarding of the revellers and reported it to the Guards. In town at that time was a **Garda O'Reilly** and he was very exact about pub closing time and related matters, such as the 'Traveller Rule'. He and **Sergeant Lupton** went to Lombard's to investigate the removal of the gates. Frances gave all the help she could, without mentioning any of the lads from her side of Cork Hill corner. She knew that Garda O'Reilly would charge them with being on the premises illegally. As it happened, the rogues who had done the mischief were from that nearer part of town and so were never found out.

Supporters travelling back from the matches in Limerick and Thurles would have a last stop at this country pub within sight of the town. Likewise after race meetings, gymkhanas and the famous Tallow Horse Fair, a final 'dismount' would be made at this piece of old Ireland.

For walkers, Lombard's was a haven on wet days, an oasis on hot days and the welcoming light at the end of the dark road for many generations over the years. Remembering great characters like **Dick Aherne, Jack Aherne, Tom Beausang, Billy Cooney, Patsy** and **Bill Dalton, Jack Delaney, John Forrest, Will Fitzgerald, Tommy Hurley, Dan Keane, Parley Ryan, Paddy O'Keeffe, Nicky Parker, Andy Lyons, Johnny Moloney, Johnny Murphy, Doll** and **Syl Redmond**, and **Cody Ryan**, brings back memories of many happy hours.

Lombards Pub

# Greens Quay – Our Playground.

This unguarded piece of grassy ground resulted from the gradual filling-in of the ships' graveyard with refuse. Some ships to end their days there were the 'Blue Jacket', 'Confidence' and the 'James Postlewaite'. Then the passing years saw the width of the public playground grow as it crept nearer to the Slob Bank corner. For generations it drew kids from all parts of town to play hurling and football between the plain netless goalposts.

Dunne's Park was the official name of this children's Croke Park, but it was always just plain Green's Quay to us. **Mikie McCarthy** was the Urban Council guardian of the swings and roundabout at the Catherine Street end of that commonage. Every night the swings would be chained together by Mikie, but there was no way of halting that great steel roundabout. So everybody climbed onto it (it could hold about twenty), to spin away the twilight of the summer evenings before reluctantly going home.

Mikie also looked after the big timber green and white shed where the tools were kept. The large seats outside, to which people came to sit and chat in good weather, were also stored inside during the winter. Familiar faces on those seats were: **Katie Duggan, Maggie Swayne, Minnie Devine, Bridget Redmond, Maggie (Harris) Griffin, Maggie Hussey, Peggy Morrison** and **Hannah O'Sullivan** (Jack the Barber's mother).

Once a year, in summer, Mikie would get help to roll the shed on timber posts into the middle of the green area in readiness for his annual free concert. A few planks on supports would serve as a stage in front of the shed and more would be spread around for seating. Most of the audience stood anyway as the local talent came together to form the show. **Johnny Walsh** with his juggling, **Mena Hallissey** with her Irish Dancers, a few local singers and then you had Mikie himself, a great accordion player. All for free. It was a local celebration of mid-summer.

On every Fairday, the animals spilled over into the green and also into nearby Dolphin's Square. This was where **Paddy O'Sullivan** had his forge and the triangle of grass in front of it would be filled with creels of screeching pigs. The **O'Callaghans, Hennessys , O'Briens, Mary Farrell**, and the **Bolands** lived in the row of houses there, going down from Watson's corner.

That same Green's Quay was where most of us first played ball with a piece of stick for a hurley, before we devised some method to accumulate a half-crown (2s. 6d.) to buy our first proper camán. Some of us would gather old aluminium kettles and teapots to sell for a few pence. Others would gather jamjars, wash them in a stream and bring them to the old L & N, where **Jack Rosney** was the Manager. We were paid a penny for a one-pound jar and twopence for a two-pound one. Just imagine all the finding, lugging and washing that went on to make the half-crown for the hurley. Then it would be off to Willie Neville's yard near Torpey's cake shop, where **Willie Sloan** of Gortroe made good hurleys, helped by **Sonny McCarthy** of Killeagh.

A large hurley was 3s. 6d. and a boy's size was 2s. 6d. Sometimes, when Willie had no small hurleys, he would give us a large one for the half-crown. We watched as he ran his keen eye over it for the last time, then a final rub of sandpaper and a happy boy got his first real hurley.

Then it was off across the road, without looking, down through Pender's Lane to put Bridie Begley's hens scattering for cover, and into Green's Quay.

Over at the goal behind John Kennedy's pub, the ash would be tested gently, not too much, as it would have to become seasoned and no clashing with other sticks was allowed for a few weeks. No heavy sliotars either ! Just a rubber ball bought from Miss Noonan's shop at 21 North Main Street for 4d.

A few years later, another hurley maker arrived from Buttevant in the person of **Jack Kelly**, to live here at Ballyvergan. Jack's camáns were fine heavy sticks, not likely to break easily. As boys we found them heavy and mainly suitable for men.

Wednesday was half-day in the Christian Brothers School to enable us to play sports. **Brothers Nelson** and **Canden** were two great promoters of the Gaelic games in our time. Br. Nelson, also our science and chant teacher, was the Hurling expert while Br. Canden was solely a football man. "*Suas leat!*' and "*Arís na nGaeil!*', would ring out to make us jump and run for the ball. We never seemed to tire and would return after tea for more.

The Street Leagues were played here between the town sections of North, Centre, South (including Strand) and Sarsfields. Sarsfield Terrace had so many boys living there as to field it's own team. What an achievement ! After all, by comparison the South had the pick of an area from the Clock Gate to Summerfield.

I feel a tinge of sadness when thinking of great promising sportsmen, who emigrated to earn their living abroad. **Bob Pomeroy, Barry O'Driscoll, Pat Leyne** and **Frank Reilly** of the South. **Paddy Phelan, Willie Kelly, Tom DeLaCour** and **Paudy White** of Sarsfields. **Tom Sullivan, Jim Aherne, Joe Izzio**, (all of Cross St.) are well remembered from the Centre, as is **Fr. Ted Hegarty**, one of the finest sportsmen to wear a Youghal and Cork jersey. Two other great footballers from the Centre were **Tom** and **John Holly**, whose parents had a chemist's shop at 85 North Main Street after Westburys. From the North division, you had **Patsy Cooney, Pat Hogan, Christy Keane, Paddy Slattery** and **Michael Piggott**. That is not all of those who left the games behind to emigrate, but space, just now, is limited.

During the Winter months, several of us played soccer at Green's Quay on week-ends, unknown to the Christian Brothers and the local G.A.A. officers. In those days, playing soccer meant a suspension of as much as twelve months from all G.A.A. games. But we took the chance quietly and got away with it. It could have been a case of people turning a blind eye to ensure having a strong team for the following year's championships.

One week-end, an under 16 soccer team was invited from Midleton to play us on a Sunday morning. The eve of the match saw us busy preparing our commonage for the game. Lime was bought at Watson's to line the field, goal posts were procured somehow out the country, and the green was transformed. The perimeterless playground never looked better and we were excited and delighted. But not everybody thought as we did.

Early the next morning, straight after Mass, we went to admire our 'Pitch'. But did we get a shock. Some begrudgers had come during the night to wreck it. The goalposts were broken, thrown down into the river, and the lines had been rubbed out. Someone did not want our soccer game against Midleton to go ahead. But we did. We got to work straight away and before the arrival of the visitors, the pitch was almost looking as well as it had on Saturday. There was one thing we could not fix, the broken cross-bars for the goals, so two lengths of rope did the trick. A big crowd turned up to watch the game, all feeling sorry for us. I cannot remember who won, which shows that it was only fun. I never learned who was responsible for that midnight mischief. What I do know is that we were just boys, playing whatever game was in season and the following week saw us back once again with our hurleys.

The Roundabout at Dunne's Park (Green's Quay) on Fair Day 1950

Youghal Brickworks 1900
*Pic: Horgans*

# Tommy Barrett – Sand Artist.

Despite suffering from constant severe shaking of his body, due to First World War shell shock, Tommy Barrett was an exceptionally good artist. He was indeed a miracle man and nobody could understand how those trembling hands could produce such beautiful pictures. The flat sand below the promenade wall was Tommy's favourite canvas. Early on Sunday morning as the tide withdrew, he would appear with a piece of stick and some stone-wash powder in different colours, to start his drawing. This powder was meant to be mixed with water for painting houses and sheds, but Tommy used it in dry form to colour his masterpieces.

As train after train full of day trippers arrived to savour the joys of the seaside, they poured out along the promenade. A glance over the wall showed the sand artist at work with his stick and colours, and the big old pennies would come flying down to him in appreciation. Sadly, the tide would return later in the day to wash away all the delightful images created by this amazing man from Cork Hill. In the meantime Tommy would have earned a good reward and would saunter off home. When tides did not permit work on the sand, he would draw on the wide footpath at South Abbey. A cluster of people peering downwards was sure to mean that Tommy Barrett, Artist Extrordinaire, was performing.

# Altar Boy Memories.

Everytime the thurible swung over and back, a fog of smoke was emitted as the ever reddening charcoal burned the incense inside the shining silver vessel. Its light chains ensured flexibility, but it was complex handling for a small altar boy. Twisted chains could spell trouble and so a small arm had to be raised high to enable them to straighten out. It seemed that the chain lengths were longer than the little altar boy could stretch and if the priest was waiting with the spoonful of incense, the small face would be as red as the charcoal. In the 1950s, altar boys were aged between 10 and 14 and would then have to 'join out' – a good Youghal expression meaning to leave or give up.

Fr. Barry (P. de B.) was in charge of the boys and practices were held before all major ceremonies like Christmas and Easter. He was a tough disciplinarian and always expected the best. On the other hand, he rewarded us with two annual outings. One was to the old Cork Opera House for the Pantomime, and the other was usually to Tramore during the Summer.

Three teams of altar boys staffed the Parish Church and each started off with six members. However, for the last year most teams had just three left. Some would have emigrated with their families while others would have found the commitment too much. A team served all the weekday ceremonies for one week in three and for the other two weeks of the cycle, just the Sunday Mass. During the 'on' week, it would be hectic. Daily 8am Mass plus extra Masses with visiting priests, especially in Summer, and evening devotions all had to be attended. In Lent and October, devotions every night called for great dedication from the team, assisted by a push from the mothers. How the mothers loved it all – lace surplices starched snow white!

As altar boys, we always had good innocent craic with the Sacristans. It was as if to balance the quiet piety of us when on duty at the far side of the sacristy wall. Sacristans remembered at Youghal Parish Church are **Paddy Long, Tommy Carey, Tommy Aher, Matty Coakley, John McCarthy, Michael Redmond** and his son, also **Michael, Florrie Coakley, Liam Ryan, Willie Shanahan, Sean O'Keefe, Liam Moynihan** and now **Liam Ryan** is back again. I remember the younger Michael Redmond had a five-shilling piece (crown), which he used to toss up when a dispute had to be settled. Sadly he died young at the age of forty-seven.

A most impressive experience for a young altar boy was to hear the rapturous singing of the packed church at the conclusion of the annual Corpus Christi Procession. The same sensation was felt on the closing night of a Mission, especially on the men's, when the heavy voices vibrated around the church as if looking for a way out. It sounded like God was making thunder in time to the singing as His contribution to this emotional expression of faith.

Mention of the Mission reminds me of serving on the evenings of the women's service. All the bikes would be resting against the wall outside the church gates and we were not allowed (thankfully) to stay on the altar during the sermon to the women. So we spent the half-hour cycling along Ashe Street on a selection of bikes, with our soutanes blowing in the slipstream. We considered this to be one of the rewards of being an altar-boy on a fine May evening, when all the other lads were off playing football.

Boys will be boys, as the saying goes, and that includes

altar-boys. Those lovely formations of wax candles waiting to be lit gave reason for competition. The two boys carrying the flaming tapers took a side of the altar each and the race was on to see whose candles would all be lighting first. At times, in the rush, a candle would die out and have to be lit again, much to the stifled amusement of the other boy. Having lit all the candles, the two boys would go to the centre of the altar, genuflect and make a quick march for the sacristy door. Inside, the sacristan would see the fast approaching two through a peep-hole and just when it appeared that they were about to crash into the door, it would open mysteriously to let them in.

How many boys can forget their kneeling alone on the altar steps for the Holy Hour of Adoration? We said our prayers for the first quarter of an hour before our minds wandered off. But the exquisite majesty of it all ! Those candles lighting in different types of holder, the many flowers with their lovely scents, and the women in the front pews wearing their Child of Mary blue gowns with white veils. After the hour had passed, how we ran down Cross Lane in escape, having done our part.

Young Altarboys at Presentation Convent 1951. Michael O'Leary, Paudy Maher & Mike Hackett

# The Man From Beyond Knockadoon

A dashing young man from beyond Knockadoon
was cycling through Dangan one evening in June,
The dance on the stage was then in full swing
And the stranger thought that he might have a swing,
So he took for his partner a maid from Kilrush
With her hair like the raven and voice like a thrush
And her smile was as bright as the sun at high noon,
Sure it dazzled THE MAN FROM BEYOND KNOCKADOON.

Tho' jealous eyes watched them on every side
As many a youth tried his envy to hide,
For Mary, she always had suitors galore,
From Inch and from Killeagh and even Lismore
And a lad from Lisgoold tried her heart for to win
And a few of Dungourney's renowned hurling men
They muttered dire threats of revenge to come soon
But they scared not THE MAN FROM BEYOND
KNOCKADOON.

He walked home with Mary when evening's soft shades
Enveloped Coolcap and the Castletown glades
And they lingered awhile on the bridge o'er the stream
As is always the case when young love's darling dream
Lights up these young hearts with it's roseate glow
As heaven's own bliss had come down here below
At Monasack Cross by the light of the moon
She parted with THE MAN FROM BEYOND KNOCKADOON.

He came here on Wednesdays and Sundays as well
And he told her the story that true lovers tell
He vowed that her eyes than the stars were more bright
That they haunted his couch and his dreamings at night
He pledged her his love and his hopes and his life
And he begged and implored her to be his own wife
At first she refused him but fearing he'd swoon She said "Yes"
to THE MAN FROM BEYOND KNOCKADOON.

Their marriage came quickly, it was not delayed
And oh the sweet tunes that the Dangan Band played
They danced and they sang in the old fashioned way
And they didn't go home 'till the dawning of day
And Mary's soft cheeks had the hue of the rose
And her voice had the ring that true happiness shows
She told all her friends she would visit them soon
With her husband, THE MAN FROM BEYOND
KNOCKADOON.

*Written by Dan O'Callaghan of Inch*

Youghal Urban District Council 1954
Back:Mick O'Sullivan, Wm.Broderick, PJ O'Gorman, Edmond Keane, Mick
Ahern. Front: Tommy Connery, Jack Daly, Susan Hurley, Eddie-Paul Lynch

# Clashmore Distillery

When approaching the scenic village of Clashmore in West Waterford, nestling in a valley beside the Blackwater, a most unusual red brick chimney-stack stands sentinel on the right-hand side, next to the stream.

At a glance it testifies to the rich heritage of this cluster of buildings with its single street. Not too long ago, the farmers queued every morning at the creamery gate, their carts loaded with milk churns. Four family bakeries catered for the village area, and 'white' bread was a treat in any country home. Going to The Village was like going to a town and Clashmore was the centre of supply for miles around.

The attractive square chimney is part of what remains of the local distillery. Apparently the whiskey made there was of great quality and kept the 'spirits' of the village folk high during the terrible trials of the time. Whatever about the quality, the quantity was subject to strict control, so that only a certain quota could be on the premises at any time. Whispers through the generations tell us that the quota was not taken seriously in Clashmore – there was ample whiskey for the villagers and country neighbours alike.

Officialdom got wind of the abundance of fun that was to be had there and revenue inspectors were dispatched several times to check the stock, but could find nothing amiss. The whiskey makers were too fast for the officials. They would quickly send word to the warehouse about the arrival of visitors, and immediately, the warehouse men would empty barrel after barrel of spirits into the passing stream. The inspectors, having spent some time in the office reading the records, would visit the warehouse to find everything perfect.

It took one young customs man to discover the secret. As he was departing from the premises, he happened to glance downstream, where he saw about twenty cattle, unable to stand, out of their minds with whiskey. The game was up.

## The Scenes above Clashmore.

To stand in the lawn at D'Loughtane,
Your heart to heaven would soar
To see those hills and winding pills
That flow to sweet Clashmore.

The Comeraghs in the distance,
The plains of Ballynatray,
And Blackwater flowing gently by
To swell the deep blue bay.

The scenes are there, but now without
The friends of boyhood years,
With whom I played, before I met
This world of bitter tears.

Some have gone to foreign lands,
More to Heaven's bright shore,
So here, O Cone, I stand alone
With the scenes above Clashmore.

*Composed by Mrs. Mary-Ellen Norris.*

# Dinny O'Shea of Dangan.

From Tuosist near Kenmare in County Kerry, in the 1920s, came a quiet but fun-loving man. Dinny O'Shea was the journey-man who made his way as far as Killeagh, before turning off towards Mount Uniacke and on to Dangan. At the time he was only seventeen and could not have realised that this was to be his homeplace for the rest of his life.

The Irish Civil-War was then not long over, as the young Irish Free State sought to establish itself. Farmers were going through lean times when Dinny came looking for work on the land. Such labour was poorly paid, there being plenty of food but no money.

Eamon de Valera's economic war with Britain was to follow, when Irish produce had no export outlet, and payment was often made to farm workers in the form of meals, board and companionship. This suited Dinny, as he sought to start a new life in this part of the country.

When he was just three years old, Dinny's mother died in childbirth. Later, when he was seven, his father, a boatbuilder, died from a severe chisel wound received at his work. Dinny had several brothers and as the boys got older, they left, one by one, to join their uncles who were boatbuilders in Boston. However, Dinny did not head for the USA and instead opted for East Cork.

In stature, he was a stocky man, of average height and very strong. His only handicap was his poor eyesight which caused him to wear very thick glasses. Dinny first came to Colemans at Mount Uniacke, doing farm work. After that, he went on to labour, as he said himself, 'at the convent' in Dangan. There was no such place but at the time he was employed by the three Beausang sisters and he had his own names for them: The Rev. Mother, The Sister in Charge, and the Yank (she had been in America for a while). This kind of humour endeared him to everyone.

Gradually, he integrated into the local scene where his clever wit also began to shine. One of his famous sayings was "I was born on the day the Titanic sank and I've drunk as much since as would refloat her". Then at the drop of a hat he would produce a pair of silver spoons from his pocket in Denis Collins' pub, in Mount Uniacke, to accompany any music; he maintained that no other spoons could ring properly.

After the Beausangs, he went to live with the Murphys in Kilcounty and was a great help and company for them. Mrs. Murphy had a daughter named Kitty with whom Dinny fell in love and for a little while things looked good. But tragedy was to strike again when sadly Kitty died at the young age of twenty-one. After that, he never looked at another girl.

A friend of his in the USA would write to him every Christmas, sending a gift of dollars, and without delay, Dinny would go to the village pub to announce "The cow has calved!". He would then clean the 'slate' and go on to order the first 'American' pint. Going home after his nourishment in the early hours of the morning, Dinny would stop outside Fitzgibbon's house to sing his thanks for their kindness to him. But they did not want his gratitude at 2 a.m.. Mrs. Fitzgibbon would put her head out the window "Go home Dinny, you have a long road before you!" "A Lao, it's not the length of it that worries me", said Dinny, "it's the width of it". Another famous saying of Dinny's was "being of sound mind, I spend every bob I have". He always said that he would follow the pint to a pound a gallon and he did.

Another story concerning Dinny O'Shea came from

back in his early years when his local pub in Mount Uniacke found drinking glasses hard to get. The publican introduced one and two pound jam jars to drink from and so Dinny would walk in and order a 'pound' of porter.

People came from far and wide to dance at Dangan's open-air stage in the 1940s where a local band provided the music under the 'Father of the Band' guidance of Thomas Kelleher. Dinny was the enthusiastic motivator behind the idea and helped to make the wooden stage. He then went on to make seats at the sides where the older people could smoke, chat and watch. There was no shortage of 'drink' from the nearby pump and cupped hands was the only way to swallow it. **Tim Fitzgibbon, Mike Draddy** and **Jack Mulcahy** would puff on their pipes while discussing farming matters on the seats. **Mossie Curtin** would play the box melodeon, **Pat Casey, Donie Kelleher** and **Joe Fitzgibbon** the violins, **Jimmy Kelleher** the accordion and on the drums you would find Dinny himself, who also doubled as Master of Ceremonies.

Many's the 'match' was made at the dances in Dangan and many's the 'craic' got serious and ended up at the altar. Dancing was every Wednesday and Sunday evenings with an extra session some Sunday afternoons. **Thomas Kelleher** had one of the few wireless sets in Dangan and would listen to Radio Luxemburg to hear the latest hit tunes and popular music. If a tune took his fancy, he would arise early the next morning, walk to Mogeely Rail Station and catch the train to Cork. Making straight for Piggot's music shop, he would buy the sheet music for his latest favourite. Back home again, the band would practice into the early hours of the morning until note perfect.

Thomas was proud of keeping his repertoire up to date and a story tells of the band playing a brand new tune called

'Buttons and Bows' one evening while the elders on the seats carried on with their conversation. Thomas gave a shout and a belt of his cap: "Whist up, can't ye hear the band playing the new tune while all ye can talk about is thinning turnips!" So good did the band become that they played regularly at dances in Dungourney and Midleton.

Dangan became famous as a place of happy gatherings for dancing and craic and Dinny O'Shea was part of it all. In true Kerry fashion, he had great grá (love) for all things Irish like traditional music and the *gaeilge*. Another of his talents was Sean Nós dancing and one evening he was called upon to give an exhibition before a large crowd. It was no bother to Dinny as he danced perfectly on top of a horse-butt, while a strong man held the shafts level.

Two years before he died, Dinny had an emotional meeting with a sister of his, Kitty, whom he had not seen since they were seven and eight years old. She had worked at the Mercy Hospital in Cork all her life and although only twenty five miles apart, neither knew the whereabouts of the other. The tears flowed freely at that reunion in the Mercy Hospital and the party went on for many hours.

In 1984, Dinny O'Shea passed quietly away. Fr. Glavin, who officiated at his funeral, was pleasantly astounded when the mourners produced a bottle of whisky at the graveside and started to tell Dinny's favourite yarns. A year later, a group of his friends erected a headstone in the tree-shaded hilltop cemetery at Dangan. Dinny O'Shea will not be forgotten for a long long time.

Dinny O'Shea
of Dangan

# The Humour of Youghal.

Humour in everyday life has always been evident in our colourful town. Alleyways, lanes and steps inspire thoughts of wit and wisdom while the great mix of traditions enables people to observe each other clearly.

All donkey carts and pony traps were moving slowly along North Main Street one day because a big man was walking ahead of them in the middle of the road. His arms were outstretched widely, nothing could pass him by and he refused to lower his limbs. In the end a farmer ran forward giving a shout to let them pass. "Don't even talk to me," was the reply "this is the width of a gap at home and I'm going into Watson's hardware to get a gate for it".

Some mannerisms around town go unnoticed completely by locals, much to the amusement of visitors. At the bus stop, one person can be heard asking another "Have you not gone home yet?" The other replies to his face "No ! Have you ?" Or one says "Do you know what I'm going to tell you ?" The reply comes "I do, what is it ?" When I am asked "Is that yourself ?" I feel like saying "No, it's somebody else".

A great compliment long ago was "You're a man beyond your appearance" – praise or not?

So many of the population in the old days could not read and write, that it was common to find people getting through life pretending that they could. One story tells of an illiterate man being so anxious to cover up his inability that every evening he would call next door to borrow the Cork Examiner, on the pretext of reading it. He would then listen to his Pye wireless set, with the wet and dry battery, and hear the news. After about an hour, he would return the 'Paper' while making a comment on the latest story. "Terrible shipwreck off the Wexford coast" and he would say and be right. It sounded like he had read the paper. Now as we all know, the Examiner goes to press early in the morning and any news after that, has to wait.

So it happened, later in the day, a terrible train crash occurred in London with thirty people dead. When my man turned on his radio that evening, having borrowed the paper, he heard about the crash. Going next door to return the Examiner he remarked "I was just reading about that terrible train crash, thirty killed". The neighbour's mouth was open for a second before he gathered his wits. "Thanks for bringing back the paper, and I can see that you won't need it tomorrow".

**Richard (Dick) Cunningham** tells of an old man he knew in his childhood. The man had just mastered the art of reading the big print in the newspaper but could make no attempt at all when confronted with handwriting. He would speak of his limited ability as "I can read READING, but I can't read WRITING "

There was a pawn shop that operated just at the north side of the Clock Gate, next to the famous Jail Steps. Men were lucky if they possessed a suit of clothes for Sundays and special occasions and all other days it was in the care of The Pawn. Then on Saturday night, when the man had got paid, one of the children would go to redeem the suit. It would be proudly displayed on Sunday and returned to the pawn on Monday to get money for food for the rest of the week. I remember remarking to an old woman about how sad that was and was surprised that she disagreed with me. "Where would we keep a suit of clothes," she said."with our big family, living in one room of a tenement building, hanging blankets on strings overnight to seperate the boys from the girls. At least the suit was safe, clean and aired in the pawn. Sure we hadn't even a wardrobe!"

Time to chat August 1965.
Mary Malone with Jack Seward in Church Street
*Pic: Joe Flores*

Dick Torpey, Dick Whelan, Gerald Ormond & Paddy Lyons.

Russells Shop 1954 *Pic Michael McKeown*

Ned Coyne, Moss Fitzgerald & John Coyne with their prize-
winning bullock at Grattan Street. *Pic Joe Hallissey*

# Going to the Pictures.

Make-believe was in the cinema. We sailed the seven seas, fought the wars, and rode the prairie. Being very young, we were not allowed to go to the night shows and so the matinees were our special time. Any wet Sunday or Wednesday afternoon found us promising to do anything for our parents in return for the fourpence admission. This would get us into the front timber seats, the 'Gods' as we knew them. Usually we prised twopence for sweets as well from our parents who were glad of a peaceful afternoon.

Youghal had two picture houses. Both were in Friar Street which seemed odd, the town being so long and the other end having nothing. Horgan's Picture Theatre was fascinating.  Entry was through two tunnels under the front screen and this gave a sense of entering a secret cavern where the magic of cinema could be enjoyed.

On the way in, the walls were covered in artistic plasterwork which portrayed the woodland and castles of the banks of the Blackwater. The artist was **Jim Horgan Senior**, the grandfather of the Horgan family and founder of the cinema. He was a pioneer of films and projectors including the famous Magic Lantern.

His experiments and inventions were years ahead of anything like them and one of his famous trick movies showed the Clock Gate dancing upside down in the street, while water flowed over it. Horgan's was built solely as a cinema and rows of seats climbed steeply from the screen to the back. It was so long that a curtain was used in wintertime to halve the hall and keep it cosier on slack nights.

**Maisie** was the outstanding character of Horgan's in

our years. I believe that she played the organ for the silent films in the earlier period. Later Maisie was the Manageress, welcoming, ushering and keeping us in check.

Across the road was the Regal cinema, owned by the **Hurst** family and managed by **Jack Finn** of Water Street, following the sudden death of Reuben Hurst. The Regal was huge in size, nearly as broad as it was long. The lovely red wall-lights cast a glow of contentment over us that assured happiness for the next two hours.

A big cheer went up as the curtain went back before the Travel-Talk short, then on to the Wonders of the World, Bugs Bunny and the serial 'Purple Monster'. At half-time that great big clamshell of adverts opened up to signify for us that it was toilet time. Off we tore to the tin shed, where we nearly wet our pants, rushing to get back inside for the 'trailers' of next week's films. Then if we hadn't called to Fred Barrett's, Bill or Bridgie Quirke's before the show, we could now go to Con Hurley's, Anna Lombard's or Loreto Rohan's for our slab toffee. Sweets like lemon drops, clove rocks and bulls' eyes were six a penny. Shopkeepers were expert at making toisins, a small square of paper rolled around the fingers and twisted shut at one end to make a triangular bag. The sweets would go in the wide mouth before turning down the flap to make a packetfull.

After the break, the main film had us glued. Then we were out by the side doors before 'The End' was gone from the screen, galloping wildly up the street, possessed out of our minds by cowboy thoughts. We ran home faster than we did from school and that was something.

During Lent, no dances were held, and all those extra people went to the cinema in addition to the usual crowd. Going to Horgan's or the Regal during those six and a half weeks meant you had to be early. The bike was the country chap's means of transport to town, light or no light, and Horgan's had a special room under the screen to hold them. I remember **Mary Murphy** of Tallow Street also gave over a room behind her shop for storing bikes. The young and not so young would arrive at Mary's on their two wheels to congregate there before taking their corduroy trouser-legs out of the socks and swaggering off downtown as if they had come by taxi. Afterwards, arriving back at Mary Murphy's shop, many of the boys would have milk and small cakes, amidst large guffawing. Untangling the bikes from each other in that back room was more craic, before they saddled up to ride out the road. Six abreast they would tear, in great glee after a night at The Pictures.

Fisherfolk at Caliso Bay: Maurice, Pats & Tom Moylan
*Pic: John Cashman*

117

# A Part of Youghal in London.

Early in 1968, **Fr. John Keogh** was based in London and realised that the number of Youghal people there justified a get-together. He contacted the Legion of Mary in the home town requesting a list of emigrants in the Greater London area. **Jack Forrest, Sean DeLaCour, Willie Walsh, Jimmy Delaney, John Roche**, with **Liam** and **Sean Noonan** were the backbone of the door-to-door enquiries to trace the exiles, especially those longest away. A sizeable list resulted and to these Fr. Keogh sent a letter requesting support and calling for people to form a committee. **Frank Aherne** and **Matty Coakley** were the first volunteers to come forward.

So it was, on the 28th. March, 1968, that Frank and Matty met at Victoria Station for the first time and walked together to the Irish Club in Eaton Square. Fr. Keogh was already there and had arranged for the first Youghal reunion to take place at that splendid venue on March 31st. 1968. Little did they know that they were to become the hub of a committee whose Association henceforth would give a sense of identity to Youghal people exiled in London. It was also to create countless new friendships whose family connections would intertwine to strengthen and even renew contact with the hometown.

Choosing the Irish Club, Eaton Square, in the centre of London was aiming high. It is a most beautiful building of the Victorian era with columns on either side of the entrance and no less than the Presidential Suite was booked for the reunion. Nobody could guess how many would turn up, although hundreds had been notified. The big day came and the early arrivals appeared at the Irish Club. More and more came from miles away to fill the Presidential Suite to capacity and later to spill over onto the stairway and into the downstairs bar. What a success! And yet more came to overflow on to the street.

An estimated 650 people attended. Time was short, too short. Old friends were meeting after years of separation, people who hadn't been home for ages were seeking out the news. Representing the Urban Council on that first occasion was the Chairman, **Gordon Good,** and from Youghal as well were **Jack Forrest** and **Sean DeLaCour**. The Youghal Association had arrived in a big way ! **Matty Coakley** was the first Chairman of the Association, **Phil Steptoe** was the Secretary and **Frank Aherne** was the first Treasurer. All have given wholehearted dedication to our exiles over the last twenty-seven years. In those earlier days, Phil worked for the BBC at Broadcasting House in Upper Regent Street and a lot of Youghal Association meetings were conveniently held in the Staff Restaurant.

Other regular patrons and committee members over the years were: **Declan McGrath, George Cashell, Mossie Walsh, Noel** and **Betty O'Connell, Tomás** and **Therese O'Connell, Eileen** and **Des Cooney, Bridie Walsh (nee Cadogan), Brendan McCarthy** (of the 'Kathleen and May'), **Bernard Bransfield, Jacky Butler, Paddy Fitzgerald** (Mall Lane), plus **Ina** and **Bella Gaule** (Town Walls). **John McCarthy** and **Betty McGrath (Doyle)** have served terms as Secretary, while **Michael O'Shea** is in his fifteenth year as Chairman. Supporters who have died since the earlier years include: **Willie Power, Tommy (Bomb) Roche**, and **Paddy Fitzgerald** (Strand).

Following the Irish Club in Eaton Square, Hayes in Middlesex became the venue for a while before the reunion moved to the Irish Centre, Camden Town, where it has been held for the past fifteen years. On the 13th. May 1995, the Annual reunion was held for the 28th time and, judging by the enthusiasm of the young newcomers, the future is assured for many more years.

3rd. Annual reunion Youghal Association held at The Spotted Dog, London 5th April 1970.
Frank Aherne, John McCarthy, Betty McGrath (Doyle), Paddy Linehan Chairman Youghal UDC, Phil Steptoe, Matty Coakley Chairman Youghal Association.
*Pic:Owen & Moroney*

All enquiries about the Youghal Association should be addressed to Frank Aherne, Secretary Youghal Association, 17 Wadham Gardens, Greenford, Middx. UB6 0BP.